Classroom Instruction
that Works
with English Language Learners

2nd Edition

Classroom Instruction *that Works*

with English Language Learners

2nd Edition

Jane D. Hill • Kirsten B. Miller

ASCD

Alexandria, VA USA

Mid-continent Research for Education and Learning
Denver, Colorado USA

1703 N. Beauregard St. • Alexandria, VA 22311-1714 USA
Phone: 800-933-2723 or 703-578-9600 • Fax: 703-575-5400
Website: www.ascd.org • E-mail: member@ascd.org
Author guidelines: www.ascd.org/write

Gene R. Carter, *Executive Director*; Mary Catherine (MC) Desrosiers, *Chief Program Development Officer*; Richard Papale, *Publisher*; Stefani Roth, *Acquisitions Editor*; Julie Houtz, *Director, Book Editing & Production*; Jamie Greene, *Editor*; Louise Bova, *Senior Graphic Designer*; Kyle Steichen, *Production Specialist*; Keith Demmons, *Desktop Publishing Specialist*

McREL
INTERNATIONAL

Mid-continent Research for Education and Learning
4601 DTC Boulevard, Suite 500
Denver, CO 80237 USA
Phone: 303-337-0990 • Fax: 303-337-3005
Website: www.mcrel.org • E-mail: info@mcrel.org

PAPERBACK ISBN: 978-1-4166-1630-6   ASCD product #114004   n11/13
Also available as an e-book (see Books in Print for the ISBNs).

Quantity discounts: 10–49 copies, 10%; 50+ copies, 15%; for 1,000 or more copies, call 800-933-2723, ext. 5634, or 703-575-5634. For desk copies: www.ascd.org/deskcopy

Library of Congress Cataloging-in-Publication Data

Hill, Jane, 1953-
 Classroom instruction that works with English language learners / Jane Hill & Kirsten Miller. — Second edition.
    pages cm
 Includes bibliographical references and index.
 ISBN 978-1-4166-1630-6 (pbk. : alk. paper) 1. Linguistic minorities—Education—United States. 2. English language—Study and teaching—Foreign speakers. 3. Language and education—United States. 4. Communication in education—United States. 5. Mainstreaming in education—United States. I. Miller, Kirsten. II. Title.
 LC3731.H554 2013
 371.829—dc23
                    2013029918

22 21 20 19 18   5 6 7 8 9 10 11 12

To my husband, Rocky Hill, who is the best chapter of my life. —Jane

---

For Arden and Finn, as all things are, and for Jeff, always. —Kirsten

Classroom Instruction *that* Works *with* English Language Learners

2nd Edition

Acknowledgments ix

Introduction xi

   1   Academic Language 1

   2   Stages of Second-Language Acquisition. 11

Part I Creating the Environment for Learning

   3   Setting Objectives and Providing Feedback. 25

   4   Reinforcing Effort and Providing Recognition 38

   5   Cooperative Learning 52

Part II Helping Students Develop Understanding

   6   Cues, Questions, and Advance Organizers 67

   7   Nonlinguistic Representations. 86

   8   Summarizing and Note Taking 99

   9   Assigning Homework and Providing Practice. 118

Part III Helping Students Extend and Apply Knowledge

   10   Identifying Similarities and Differences 135

   11   Generating and Testing Hypotheses 150

Conclusion. 159

Appendix A: The Academic Language Framework 161

Appendix B: Thinking Language Matrix 162

Appendix C: Template for Planning
Language Objectives. 164

Appendix D: Sample Graphic Organizers. 165

References 171

Index. 175

About the Authors 181

Acknowledgments

We gratefully acknowledge the following Nebraska educators who piloted the Academic Language Framework and the process for identifying the vocabulary, grammar, and sentence starters related to math and science standards:

Angela Bergman

Penny Businga

Rosemary Cervantes

Dayna Derichs

Pam Erixon

Jennifer Gaston

Thomas Harrington

Jewel Hoxworth

Gulnora Isaeva

Jacquetta Johnson

Kim Juranek

Ronald Kaspar Jr.

Mary Lamken

Candy List

Denine Marshall

Courtney Matulka

Rebecca Mussack

Jennifer Nicholson

Cyndi Reed

Nancy Rowch

Valerie Schovanec

Clarissa Schumacker

Terri Schuster

Matthew Scott

Megan Septak

Nancy Sivils

Debra Skokan

Emily Smith

Rebecca Sosalla

Marian Wallen

Wendy Wendt

Without the ingenious thinking of our former McREL colleague Cynthia Björk, the Thinking Language Matrix would not appear in this book. Another former colleague, Candy Hyatt, was instrumental in developing the examples in the Thinking Language Matrix that appear throughout this book. Our sincere thanks to these friends and colleagues.

Without the seminal work of Robert Marzano, Debra Pickering, and Jane Pollock, we would not have been able to write *Classroom Instruction That Works with English Language Learners* (Hill & Flynn, 2006), *Classroom Instruction That Works with English Language Learners Facilitator's Guide* (Hill & Björk, 2008a), and *Classroom Instruction That Works with English Language Learners Participant's Workbook* (Hill & Björk, 2008b). This second edition of *Classroom Instruction That Works with English Language Learners* builds on the work of our McREL colleagues Ceri Dean, Elizabeth Hubbell, Howard Pitler, and Bj Stone, who wrote the second edition of *Classroom Instruction That Works* (2012).

We gratefully acknowledge Ceri Dean—our *Classroom Instruction That Works* guru, who shared with us her vast knowledge of the strategies and her inimitable good humor during the writing and review process—and Renée Regnier, who guided us through the logistical details that come with preparing a manuscript.

A big thank you to our friends and colleagues at ASCD—Laura Lawson, Stefani Roth, and Jamie Greene—for their support, guidance, and edits.

This book reflects many years of consulting with state departments of education and providing professional development here and abroad. All those countless experiences helped shape the thinking and examples contained in this book. We hope you find them valuable.

Last, but not least, we thank our families for their ongoing love and support.

Introduction

Language has always been the medium of instruction. As teachers, our automatic use of English helps us to create or produce something new for students. We can create stories, produce explanations, construct meaning when we read, and help students make meaningful connections—all just by opening our mouths.

However, the demographics in our classrooms have changed, and students' language learning is no longer the sole responsibility of the English as a Second Language teacher. As of the 2010–2011 school year, English language learners made up 13 percent of the student population nationwide (U.S. Department of Education, n.d.). It's not only students learning English who may need language development; it's also native-born students who enter school without a firm foundation in English language development at a level necessary to access curriculum content. These students may come from lower socioeconomic or other high-risk environments, where they have fewer verbal interactions with peers or parents and other caregivers, which can result in substandard academic language development. These students are similar to some English language learners because, although they are conversationally proficient, such proficiency is not the only language competency needed for academic success.

What do regular classroom teachers need to know to become better supporters of language development? This second edition of *Classroom Instruction That Works with English Language Learners* combines the language development tools used in McREL's training programs with the newly energized strategies from the second edition of *Classroom Instruction That Works* (Dean, Hubbell,

Pitler, & Stone, 2012) to provide a comprehensive instructional guide for mainstream teachers of students acquiring English and other students in need of language development.

What Is Classroom Instruction That Works?

Classroom Instruction That Works describes nine categories of instructional strategies that have a high likelihood of improving student achievement. In 2001, McREL presented the research supporting these categories in the first edition of *Classroom Instruction That Works* (Marzano, Pickering, & Pollock, 2001). In 2012, based on updated research and more than a decade of intervening field experience, our colleagues at McREL wrote the second edition of *Classroom Instruction That Works* (Dean et al., 2012).

Since the first edition of *Classroom Instruction That Works with English Language Learners* was published in 2006 (Hill & Flynn), we've learned a lot about how to foster higher-order thinking and learning for students with limited English proficiency. With this second edition, we're applying that deeper understanding to each of the nine categories of strategies.

Organization of the Book

In the first edition of *Classroom Instruction That Works,* the strategies were organized by the magnitude of their effect size. Many readers took this presentation as a de facto rank ordering, encouraging them to focus on the first several strategies while more or less neglecting the others. As a result, the second edition of *Classroom Instruction That Works* reorganized the nine instructional categories into an instructional planning framework that focuses on key aspects of teaching and learning. We use that same framework in this second edition of *Classroom Instruction That Works with English Language Learners*:

I. Creating the Environment for Learning
- Setting Objectives and Providing Feedback
- Reinforcing Effort and Providing Recognition
- Cooperative Learning

II. Helping Students Develop Understanding
- Cues, Questions, and Advance Organizers

- Nonlinguistic Representations

- Summarizing and Note Taking

- Assigning Homework and Providing Practice

III. Helping Students Extend and Apply Knowledge
- Identifying Similarities and Differences

- Generating and Testing Hypotheses

Students learning English as another language need explicit instruction in acquiring academic English. Chapters 1 and 2 provide background information on academic language and the stages of language acquisition. What should we do differently when emerging second-language learners and others who need language development are part of the regular education classroom? In this book, we provide you with tools to apply the *Classroom Instruction That Works* strategies with your students learning English, including prompts, activities, and updated classroom examples.

Each chapter from 3 through 11 addresses one of the nine categories of research-based strategies for increasing student achievement. These chapters include action-oriented content that more deeply reflects practical ways to apply the strategies to instructing English language learners and others in need of language development, and they offer tips on how teachers can foster English language proficiency as part of subject-matter instruction. Because many second-language learners are in mainstream classrooms for the entire school day, teachers should support language development and content by applying the recommendations offered in this book.

New in This Edition

New to this second edition of *Classroom Instruction That Works with English Language Learners* are the Thinking Language Matrix and sections that offer opportunities to develop oral academic language (using our Academic Language

Framework). In addition, there are tips for teaching and examples aligned to the Common Core State Standards and the Next Generation Science Standards.

The Thinking Language Matrix

The Thinking Language Matrix aligns the higher-order thinking skills of Bloom's taxonomy to the stages of second-language acquisition for each specific strategy. The matrix provides a tool for challenging English language learners at all levels of thinking and across all stages of second-language acquisition. It illustrates that a lack of English language proficiency does not necessarily indicate a corresponding lack of higher-order thinking skills. The alignment of stages of second-language acquisition with higher-order thinking effectively encourages new, and more rigorous, approaches to instruction. This approach provides opportunities for second-language learners to think and interact with knowledge at more sophisticated levels.

Educators using the Thinking Language Matrix have experienced epiphanies when they realize that even beginning-level English language learners can work at all levels of higher-order thinking. When students are acquiring English as a new language together with new content, the Thinking Language Matrix provides educators with a framework for thinking about students' stages of English proficiency in conjunction with what students are expected to accomplish in tasks based on Bloom's taxonomy. Some educators have suggested using the Thinking Language Matrix as a guideline for addressing rigor with students acquiring English as another language.

Opportunities to develop oral academic language

Research strongly supports the need for English language learners to develop rich oral academic language as a precursor for reading and writing proficiently in English (e.g., August & Shanahan, 2006; Fillmore & Snow, 2000; Saunders & Goldenberg, 2010; Saunders & O'Brien, 2006; Walqui, 2010; Williams & Roberts, 2011). For each strategy, we describe how to incorporate opportunities to develop oral academic language into subject-area content. Teachers of English language learners and others in need of language development recognize the need to support the rich oral academic language of instructional content but might not be sure about how to make it happen. We offer concrete ways to set the stage for productive academic talk that are aligned to each of the categories of McREL's research-based instructional strategies.

Examples aligned to standards

As noted in our description of the Thinking Language Matrix, lower-level language skills are not equivalent to lower-level thinking skills. Similarly, the increased rigor demanded by the Common Core State Standards and the Next Generation Science Standards does not mean that linguistically diverse students can't meet these standards. Throughout this book, we provide the tools needed to incorporate academic language into content and to address the higher-order thinking skills called for in the current generation of standards. As an additional support, we provide specific examples aligned to the standards using the Academic Language Framework, a tool for infusing language-development standards into content. The framework provides a template for thinking about the language of content and a sequence of steps that will help you select key vocabulary words and grammar concepts and design content-based sentence starters that help students engage in productive academic talk.

Tips for teaching

At the end of Chapters 3 through 11, we pull everything together with a list of tips for teaching students in need of language development. The goal is to make each strategy work for *all* students, no matter what their stage of language proficiency.

A Note on Acronyms

In this book, we show you how to involve culturally and linguistically diverse students, at all stages of second-language acquisition, in higher-order thinking. These students are in our charge, and it's our responsibility to help them reach the highest levels of learning possible. We sincerely believe that these students are children first and English language learners second.

To avoid reducing students in need of language development to a label, we have chosen not to refer to them in the acronym-rich language of the field:

ELL, LEP, CLD, or ESL. Rather, we use a number of other descriptors, such as "students acquiring English" and "second-language learners."

As we run through all of the acronyms used to refer to children (and adults) in the fields of education, psychology, mental health, and social services, we know that we wouldn't want to be known simply as a series of capital letters. It is our hope that avoiding the use of acronyms in this book will help us keep our collective focus on our students as individuals.

1

Academic Language

In the 1980s, the field of second-language acquisition was widely influenced by theories developed by Krashen and Terrell (1983) and Cummins (1984). Krashen proposed five hypotheses to explain how another language is acquired, and Cummins introduced us to the differences between basic interpersonal communicative skills (BICS), or conversational language, and cognitive academic language proficiency (CALP), or what we now know as academic language. (We explore these concepts further in Chapter 2.) More recently, Anstrom and her colleagues (2010) delivered the 50-page *Review of the Literature on Academic English: Implications for K–12 English Language Learners*, which documents the research that contributes to our understanding of academic English and how it is taught and learned.

In other words, this is a complex concept and one addressed by many scholars. In this chapter, we sort through the research to investigate language functions and structures; highlight what it means for students to use productive accountable talk and "sound like a book"—that is, to express their reasoning using academic language; and show how function, structure, and discourse fit into a framework that will help teachers identify the content-area academic language needed to explicitly teach their students.

Determining Language Functions and Structures

Language can best be understood as action, rather than form or function alone (Walqui, 2012); students learn to do things with language when they

1

participate in meaningful activities that engage and challenge them. Students will learn more English when engaged in the action of talking with other students than through typical teacher-directed activities designed solely to deliver content. Participation in oral activities has a dual purpose: it develops conceptual understanding and increases language use.

Fathman, Quinn, and Kessler (1992) point out that "language functions are specific uses of language for accomplishing certain purposes" (p. 12). In other words, the function of language is dependent on its purpose in a given lesson. For example, are students using it to describe? Explain? Persuade? Language *structure*, by contrast, refers to the words themselves and how they are strung together into phrases and sentences.

Language functions

Language functions exist in both oral and written communication. In real-life conversations, we may need to describe our weekend, explain how to get to a restaurant, or persuade a friend to help us with a project. Knowing how to use these language functions allows us to participate fully in these conversations. In school, we teach students to write for a variety of purposes. For example, we might ask a student to describe an animal in a report, explain how to plant a seed in a procedural manner, or persuade classmates to recycle.

A powerful reciprocal relationship links talking and writing. Talking allows students to develop ideas and language they can use while writing, and writing allows them to develop ideas and language they can express orally.

When teachers ask students to write for a variety of purposes and across different genres, students learn language functions. According to Gibbons (1991), a multitude of language functions for speaking occur in the classroom each day, including the following:

- Agreeing and disagreeing
- Apologizing
- Asking for assistance or directions
- Asking for permission
- Classifying
- Commanding/Giving instructions
- Comparing
- Criticizing
- Denying
- Describing
- Evaluating
- Explaining
- Expressing likes and dislikes
- Expressing obligation
- Expressing position
- Hypothesizing
- Identifying
- Inferring
- Inquiring/Questioning
- Planning and predicting
- Refusing
- Reporting
- Sequencing
- Suggesting
- Warning
- Wishing and hoping

Language structures

The term *language structure* refers to what students say: the phrasing, key words, and grammatical usage that students acquiring English will need in order to participate in a lesson. Like language functions, language structures exist in both oral and written communication. Whereas language function is the "purpose" for talking, language structure refers to the "what"—the elements that culturally and linguistically diverse students will need to help them get the English out of their mouths.

To identify the language structure that accompanies language function, teachers should think in terms of the following elements:

- Sentence starters
- Key words or vocabulary
- Minilessons on using grammar to communicate meaning (keep in mind that grammar should be taught for practical use in authentic contexts—not as isolated rules)

Returning to the example of the real-life conversation mentioned earlier, when we describe our weekend, we might naturally say something such as "Over the weekend, I went to the zoo. I went to the park. I cleaned my kitchen. I also walked my dog." Consider the overall phrasing necessary to communicate this information. Appropriate sentence starters could include "Over the weekend, I went to ___" or "I ___ my___." Key words could include the names of places and things such as *park, zoo, dog,* and *kitchen*. A grammar minilesson could focus on the use of past-tense verbs or the idiomatic expression *over the weekend*. Let's take a look at some examples that illustrate the language functions, structures, and objectives that need to be addressed in a lesson.

Example 1: Sentence starters

Subject: Language Arts
Content Objective: To learn how to express persuasive opinions
Language Objective: To use sentence starters such as "I think" and "In my opinion" to form opinions

The language function is *persuading* because the lesson involves expressing opinions in order to persuade. The language structure is using the sentence starters "I think" and "In my opinion." The language objective is therefore using these starters to express opinions.

Example 2: Key words

Subject: Mathematics
Content Objective: To comprehend the differences between two or more polygons
Language Objective: Using *more than* and *less than* to compare polygons

The language function includes both *identifying* and *comparing* in a two-step process. Students will need to be able to identify each polygon and then say how the polygons compare to one another.

Because students will need to understand comparative structures such as *greater than* and *less than*, the language objective becomes using these phrases to compare polygons.

Example 3: Minilesson

Subject: Social Studies
Content Objective: To understand the period of the 1920s and the women's rights movement
Language Objective: To learn contractions in order to make comparisons

Because students will be comparing what women could and couldn't do—and what they did and didn't do—in the 1920s, they will need the language function of *comparing*. The language structure is contractions. The language objective is to learn contractions in order to make comparisons.

Developing Oral Academic Language: Sound Like a Book

Conversational language differs from academic language. Conversational language is the informal, chatty way of talking that students use with family and friends, whereas academic language is language used at school and characterized by longer, more complex sentences that contain vocabulary less frequently heard than the vocabulary in everyday spoken English.

Each content area includes particular discourse, or ways of talking. For example, passive voice is common in science, because science is objective and we refer to scientific phenomena by focusing on the action. For example, "experiments were conducted by the scientists." Students in the process of learning English need teacher modeling of this type of language use and time to interact with others and use the passive voice when they "talk science."

Just as science is known for passive voice, history is known for chronological discourse, because it's written according to a time sequence. Certain transitional words, also known as signal words, accompany historical text and are used by authors to link ideas together. The language of time sequences includes words such as *initially, followed by, immediately, afterward, meanwhile,* and *eventually.* We want students to use these words when discussing history in the classroom. Mathematics, on the other hand, focuses on generalizations and principles, using academic language such as *if . . . then, for instance, generally, it could be argued that,* and *therefore.*

When we ask students to use the language of science, history, or math, we're asking them to "sound like a book." Students may initially need to have their learning scaffolded. Teachers can first ask students to verbalize something as if they were their parents or as if they were the principal. Next, students could be asked to sound like a scientist, historian, or mathematician. In analyzing how professionals speak, students should be led to recognize that such speech involves longer, more complex sentences and uses higher-level vocabulary than is common in everyday speech. The use of signal words contributes to creating longer compound sentences.

The Academic Language Framework

Given the growing numbers of English language learners and other students in need of language development in our classrooms, simply teaching content is no longer enough. Subject-matter teachers are being called upon to address the academic language that accompanies their content.

The Academic Language Framework (see Appendix A for a blank template) offers a structure for deciphering the language demands of content. Here's how to use the framework:

1. "Go to the balcony"—step back and get a sense of the big picture—and observe your students when they're engaged in productive accountable talk. They may be discussing what they have read or are going to write but aren't yet engaged in the actual task of reading or writing. For example, while addressing a 5th grade English Language Arts standard from the Common Core State Standards (CCSS.ELA-Literacy.R.L5.5), a teacher might ask his or her students to sequence events in one of the chapters from *Sarah, Plain and Tall* by Patricia MacLachlan. This task is recorded in the Task portion of the template (see Figure 1.1).

FIGURE 1.1
Academic Language Framework for a 5th Grade English Language Arts Lesson

Task	Exemplars	Academic Language			
		Function of Language	Vocabulary	Grammar	Sentence Starter(s)
Sequence events in one of the chapters.	"First, the sky grew dark and everyone went to the storm shelter. While they were in the barn, Sarah remembered some impor-tant memen-tos in the house. After-wards, Caleb noticed the colors of the sky were the same as the ocean Sarah described."	sequencing	*mementos*	adverbs of time	First, _____. Next, _____. Meanwhile, _____. Afterwards, _____.

2. Write down what you expect students to say as they engage in discussion. What rich oral academic language can they use as they sequence events? Record one or two examples in the Exemplars section. In 5th grade, English-proficient students could be expected to say, "First, the sky grew dark and everyone went to the storm shelter. While they were in the barn, Sarah remembered some important mementos in the house. Afterwards, Caleb noticed the colors of the sky were the same as the ocean Sarah described."

3. Identify the language function word in the task, and record it in the Function of Language section of the template. Examples of language function words are *compare, explain, describe, interpret, justify, evaluate, sequence, analyze,* and *create*. (The template shows the verbal noun *sequencing*, derived from the language function word *sequence* in the Task column.)

4. Decide what English-language-learning students need in order to engage in this level of academic talk. Record these items in the appropriate parts of the template: Vocabulary, Grammar, and Sentence Starter(s).

Vocabulary: key words needed to engage in the standard; for example, *mementos*.

Grammar: grammatical structures and parts of speech; for example, adverbs of time.

Sentence Starters: sentence starters students will find helpful; for example, *First, _____; Next, _____; Meanwhile, _____; and Afterwards, _____.*

In Chapter 3, we demonstrate how to use the framework to set language objectives. Chapter 5 illustrates how to use the framework to incorporate cooperative learning structures while implementing Common Core State Standards in mathematics. In Chapters 7, 8, 10, and 11, we apply the framework to the Next Generation Science Standards and the Common Core State Standards via the strategies of nonlinguistic representations, summarizing and note taking, identifying similarities and differences, and generating and testing hypotheses.

The Thinking Language Matrix

Another way to help teachers think about the language that students need in order to be successful is to use McREL's second-language acquisition and taxonomy matrix (see Figure 1.2)—what we call the Thinking Language Matrix (Hill & Björk, 2008a, 2008b). This matrix aligns the levels of thinking from Bloom's taxonomy (Bloom, Engelhart, Furst, Hill, & Krathwohl, 1956) to the stages of second-language learning. (For this book, we use Bloom's original taxonomy from 1956. Although there has been a revision and other taxonomies have since been developed, the original Bloom's is most familiar to the majority of teachers. When we present new information, such as aligning stages of second-language acquisition with the taxonomy levels, starting with the familiar can help avoid misapprehensions.)

Using the matrix, teachers can address the language demands in their lessons as follows:

1. Identify the taxonomic level of the task you are asking students to perform (Knowledge, Comprehension, Application, Analysis, Synthesis, Evaluation).

2. Ask yourself what you would expect your proficient students to say and do as they participate in the activity. Record this in the Intermediate/Advanced Fluency column. You'll want to begin with this stage and work backward because native English speakers or proficient English language learners will meet the description of this stage, and you can use those speakers to gauge other students' placement.

3. Think about a student you teach who is at one of the earlier stages of second-language acquisition. What is this student going to need in order to be able to participate in a small-group discussion? What is the purpose of the discussion (e.g., to describe, explain, compare, interpret)? What language structure will this student need? Record this in the middle column.

4. Return to the verbs in the taxonomy level and think about your Preproduction students (see Chapter 2 for more information on the stages of second language acquisition). Because they can think at the taxonomic level but cannot verbalize the answer, what can those students do to participate effectively? Can they sketch, symbolize, or illustrate? Record a demonstration in the Preproduction column.

See Appendix B for a blank template of the matrix. The example that follows explains how a teacher might use the process to create the completed matrix shown in Figure 1.2.

The English Language Proficiency Development Framework developed by the Council of Chief State School Officers (2012) offers helpful ways to think about the academic language embedded in the Common Core math standards. For example, Common Core Mathematical Practice Standard 1 expects students to make sense of problems and persevere in solving them (Council of Chief State School Officers, 2010). At a kindergarten level, a student might be asked to "explain data," which would be found under Levels of Thinking in Comprehension. With this in mind, a teacher might expect students to say "There are more red blocks than blue blocks because this set has eight and the

FIGURE 1.2
Thinking Language Matrix Example

Levels of Thinking and Language Functions	Tiered Thinking Across Stages of Second-Language Acquisition				
	Language moves from simple to complex in grammatical tenses, forms, vocabulary, etc.				
Level of thinking and academic language required for any task; move from concrete recall to more complex, abstract levels.	WORD ⟶ MODEL ⟶ EXPAND ⟶ SOUND LIKE A BOOK				
	Preproduction: nonverbal response	**Early Production:** one-word response	**Speech Emergence:** phrases or short sentences	**Intermediate Fluency:** longer and more complex sentences	**Advanced Fluency:** near native
Comprehension classify, describe, discuss, explain, express, identify, indicate, locate, recognize, report, restate, review, select, translate	The student represents which set has more/less by arranging the blocks.	Sentence starter: There are ___ red blocks than blue blocks. OR Key vocabulary: *more, less, equal*		"There are more red blocks than blue blocks because this set has eight and the other set has six." "These two sets are equal because they both have seven blocks."	

other set has six" or "These two sets are equal because they both have seven blocks." The teacher records these examples in the Intermediate/Advanced column. The teacher would then think about the purpose of the small-group discussion and conclude that students are describing how sets are formed. Students then need sentence starters, such as "There are _____ red blocks than blue blocks," or the specific vocabulary words *more, less,* and *equal.* This is recorded in the Early Production/Speech Emergence column. The teacher may decide that the Preproduction students can represent sets with *more* or *less* by using red and blue blocks (manipulatives) to represent the data and compare the number of blocks in each set. This demonstration is recorded in the Preproduction column.

Examples of the Thinking Language Matrix appear in each of the following chapters to illustrate how to engage students at all stages of second-language acquisition in the levels of Bloom's taxonomy.

2

Stages of Second-Language Acquisition

Anyone who has been around a child learning his or her first language knows that the process happens in stages—first understanding, then one-word utterances, then two-word phrases, and so on. Second-language acquisition is similar to native-language acquisition in some, though not all, ways. Stephen Krashen and Tracy Terrell first explored these stages of second-language acquisition in their 1983 book, *The Natural Approach*. They identified five predictable stages through which students advance when they are acquiring a second language: Preproduction, Early Production, Speech Emergence, Intermediate Fluency, and Advanced Fluency. Other sources, including English language proficiency assessments, may use different terminology for similar stages. For example, the ACCESS for ELLs (Assessing Comprehension and Communication in English State-to-State for English Language Learners) language exam developed by World-Class Instructional Design and Assessment (WIDA) identifies students as "Entering" rather than "Preproduction." Figure 2.1 summarizes the five stages of language acquisition and shows some appropriate prompts and tiered (stage-appropriate) questions to use for each stage of second-language acquisition. By knowing the stages and appropriate questions, teachers can engage students at the correct level of discourse.

FIGURE 2.1

Stages of Second-Language Acquisition and Tiered Questions

Stage	Characteristics	Approximate Time Frame	Tiered Questions (Prompts)
Preproduction	The student • Has minimal comprehension without scaffolds. • Does not verbalize. • Nods *yes* and *no*. • Draws and points.	0–6 months	• Show me . . . • Circle the . . . • Where is . . . ? • Who has . . . ?
Early Production	The student • Has limited comprehension without support. • Produces one- or two-word responses. • Participates using key words and familiar phrases. • Uses present-tense verbs.	6 months–1 year	• Yes/no questions • Either/or questions • *Who, what,* and *how many* questions
Speech Emergence	The student • Has good comprehension. • Can produce simple sentences. • Makes grammatical and pronunciation errors. • Frequently misunderstands jokes.	1–3 years	• Why . . . ? • How . . . ? • Explain . . . • Questions requiring a phrase or short-sentence answers
Intermediate Fluency	The student • Has excellent comprehension. • Makes few grammatical errors.	3–5 years	• What would happen if . . . ? • Why do you think . . . ? • Questions requiring more than a one-sentence response
Advanced Fluency	The student has a near-native level of speech.	5–7 years	• Decide if . . . • Retell . . .

Source: Information adapted from *The Natural Approach: Language Acquisition in the Classroom,* by S. D. Krashen and T. Terrell, 1983, Oxford: Pergamon.

In second-language acquisition, the Preproduction stage lasts from zero to six months and is also known as "the silent period," because it's possible that you won't hear students speak any English at all. The next level, Early Production, is similar to when children first begin to speak in their native language—students begin using single words or two-word phrases, yes/no responses, names, and repetitive language patterns (e.g., "How are you?"). Think about your own children, or children you've been around, as they began to move past one-word responses and combine words into sentences. Those sentences aren't always grammatically correct or structurally accurate, and the same will be true for English language learners who are in the Early Production stage. At the Speech Emergence stage, students are able to say simple sentences, such as "I walked home." Eventually, at the Intermediate Fluency stage, students can use sentences of increasing length and complexity until finally, at the Advanced Fluency stage, they demonstrate a near-native level of fluency.

Traditionally, the stages of second-language acquisition were solely the domain of teachers of English as a Second Language. As a result of mainstreaming, we can now find students learning English in almost every classroom. In addition, the No Child Left Behind Act of 2001 requires that students who are acquiring English demonstrate progress in both content knowledge and English language proficiency, which means that all teachers need to understand students' stages of second-language acquisition and support academic language development in addition to content knowledge.

Why is it important for all teachers to possess this knowledge? Knowing the level of language acquisition allows you to work within each student's "zone of proximal development"—that area between what the student is capable of at the moment and the point you want the student to reach next (Vygotsky, 1978). You can work in a student's zone of proximal development by scaffolding language development or by providing the support students need as they progress. Scaffolding is essentially a way to nudge a student toward a higher level of performance. With language development, this can be done by modeling correct grammar or pronunciation, asking challenging questions, or providing direct instruction. For example, students in the Preproduction stage will be successful at stage-appropriate tasks such as pointing to, finding, or circling a picture. However, you can scaffold further development by supporting them as they attempt tasks characteristic of the Early Production stage, such as answering yes/no or either/or questions or providing one-word responses. This approach provides realistic expectations, reinforces current language skills, and encourages and strengthens future language learning.

Similarly, you may reinforce the second-language learner's response and ask the student to add a word to the phrase and restate it or to use a word to connect two short phrases. Again, you are meeting the student at his or her current language level and extending an opportunity for that student to move forward in his or her language acquisition.

When asked how knowing the stages of second-language acquisition has helped her with students who are acquiring English as another language, a high school teacher in Wyoming noted that before learning the stages, she believed that a recently arrived sophomore student from Mexico didn't like her because he hadn't spoken to her. The teacher hadn't realized that the recent arrival was in the Preproduction stage, or "silent period," of language acquisition. Many teachers with whom we've worked have also noted that understanding the stages helps them adjust their expectations accordingly (for example, by not expecting a written essay from a Preproduction student or by asking a Speech Emergence student to point to a picture rather than answer using a short sentence).

By knowing each student's stage of second-language acquisition, teachers can work within the zone of proximal development—the gap between what students can do independently and what they can reach with the aid of others. This approach helps us avoid "lifers" in the English as a Second Language program by always moving students toward the next stage of language acquisition.

Asking Tiered Questions

Many classroom teachers haven't received adequate training to meet the needs of culturally and linguistically diverse students in their regular education classrooms (de Jong & Harper, 2005). With that in mind, where's a good place to start supporting language attainment alongside subject matter knowledge and skills? Let's begin with tiered questions, a strategy in which a teacher asks a question associated with a student's stage of second-language acquisition. The last column of Figure 2.1 displays possible teacher prompts or tiered questions for each stage of second-language acquisition, allowing teachers to engage students at the correct level of output.

TRY THIS: Ask tiered questions.

A teacher from Newport News, Virginia, tried tiered questions with Leonardo, a 3rd grade Hispanic student who previously said very little. Here is her description of what happened:

"Prior to today's lesson, I identified Leonardo's stage of second-language acquisition and noted the prompts that I needed to use. He fell between Early Production and Speech Emergence. I used some of the suggested sentence starters and tiered questions coupled with me sometimes pointing at specifics in the illustrations and text. His responses were almost immediate and more frequent. Additionally, I found that the English-speaking students' responses reflected a better understanding of the lesson. I was absolutely thrilled!"

Although aligning the questions you ask with the correct stage of language acquisition is important, as we noted earlier, occasionally asking a question from the next level can help students progress. Here's the guideline: ask students a question at their appropriate level of acquisition, but every so often (for example, every 1 in 10 questions) ask a question one level above. If we look at Figure 2.1, this means that Preproduction students can be asked to point or show but occasionally asked a question from the Early Production stage (such as a yes/no or an either/or question). Asking an occasional Early Production question will help transition students to that next stage.

High levels of student engagement are "a robust predictor of student achievement and behavior in school" (Klem & Connell, 2004, p. 262). By frequently asking tiered questions throughout a lesson, teachers can increase students' engagement with the content and provide opportunities for them to practice their new language at the same time. In addition, when classrooms include students along the whole continuum of second-language acquisition—from Preproduction to Advanced Fluency—asking tiered questions helps teachers engage *all* of their students.

Example

> **Tiered Questions in Elementary Science**
> **Grade Level:** K–2
> **Strategy:** Ask questions appropriate to students' stages of language acquisition.

A 1st grade class is sorting items into two groups: items that are affected by magnets and items that are not affected by magnets. As the teacher circulates among the small groups engaged in this classifying activity, she asks the following types of tiered questions:

Preproduction—Ask questions that students can answer by pointing: "Show me where this marble goes." Ask a question from the next tier: "Can the wooden block go here?"

Early Production—Ask questions that students can answer with one-word responses: "Did all of the items respond the same way to the magnet?" Ask a question from the next tier: "Why does the pen belong here?"

Speech Emergence—Ask *why* and *how* questions that students can answer with a short sentence: "Why can the magnet move the bolt?" Ask a succeeding question: "Why do you think the magnet can lift the paper clip but not the pebble?"

Intermediate Fluency—Ask "What would happen if . . ." and "Why do you think . . ." questions: "What would happen if we wrapped the magnet in paper?" Help move students to the next level by asking them to restate what they said using a higher-level vocabulary word, such as *repel*.

Advanced Fluency—Ask students to "sound like a scientist," and have them describe the property that determines whether an object can be moved by a magnet by using words such as *opposing*, *attracted*, and *repel*.

Tiered Thinking Across Stages of Second-Language Acquisition

Tiered questions help us think about the relationship between the questions we ask and students' levels of language acquisition. How might we think about the questions we ask and the level of thinking those questions require from our students who are culturally and linguistically diverse?

In a seminal study of bilingual education programs, Ramirez (1992) found that in all of the programs studied (including immersion and early- and late-exit transitional programs), teachers tended to ask low-level questions. In fact, in more than half of their interactions, students did not produce any oral language; when they did, they engaged in simple recall. Ramirez's study may reflect many teachers' beliefs that Preproduction and Early Production students can't answer a high-level question because the most they can do is point or give a one-word response. Even though Preproduction students may respond best by pointing and Early Production students benefit from one-word response questions, teachers should avoid asking only questions that require simple recall of knowledge. An emerging English user's limited verbal output does not mean the student has limited cognition. Teachers should ask English-language-learning students high-level questions regardless of their level of language acquisition.

Bloom's taxonomy (Bloom et al., 1956) provides a structure for categorizing questions' levels of abstraction so we can distinguish between questions that require lower-level thinking and those that require higher-level thinking. The taxonomy can be ordered from most to least complex levels of thinking, with Evaluation (judging the accuracy of information) at the highest level and Knowledge (recall) at the lowest:

- Evaluation
- Synthesis
- Analysis
- Application
- Comprehension
- Knowledge

In the example that follows, we look more closely at how a teacher might engage Preproduction students in all levels of critical thinking.

Example

Critical Thinking for English Language Learners	
Grade Level: Secondary	
Strategy: Enable Preproduction students to work at all levels of Bloom's taxonomy.	

A secondary science teacher wants Preproduction students to practice, review, and apply what they've been learning about parts of plants and their functions. Here is a chart that illustrates how Preproduction students can work at all levels of Bloom's taxonomy:

Evaluation	Assess the correctness of a moveable biome model. Show understanding by rearranging parts as necessary.
Synthesis	Plan and construct dioramas or collages to show seasons in a forest biome.
Analysis	Categorize types of plants found in desert and alpine tundra biomes using pictures and labels.
Application	Graph how tall plants get under specific conditions.
Comprehension	Match parts of a plant to their functions.
Knowledge	Label and order the steps of the plant cycle. Respond to the teacher's request to point to, gesture for, draw, or match icons for the steps of the plant cycle.

As we've noted, there's a tendency to believe that students in the initial stages of language acquisition can answer only low-level questions and that those in the advanced stages are more likely to be able to answer high-level questions. However, as the science example shows, the relationship between the levels of thinking and the stages of second-language acquisition is not a simple side-by-side alignment. Rather, this relationship is better illustrated with a set of axes that represent the idea that students learning English can

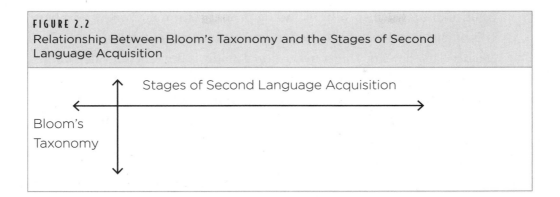

FIGURE 2.2
Relationship Between Bloom's Taxonomy and the Stages of Second Language Acquisition

work at all levels of higher-order thinking, regardless of their level of English language acquisition.

Hill and Bjork's (2008a, 2008b) Thinking Language Matrix, which was introduced in Chapter 1, reflects this relationship. In the chapters that follow, we present examples of how this matrix can be used with each category of instructional strategies. Our goal is to highlight the point that if we direct and maintain English language learners' engagement at the lowest levels of *thinking*, then we confine them to the lowest levels of *learning*. By using the Thinking Language Matrix, mainstream teachers can keep all levels of language learners engaged at all levels of thinking.

Reasonable Time Frames for Passing Through the Stages

How long should it take an English language learner to pass through the stages of second-language acquisition? According to Thomas and Collier's (1997) comprehensive study, under the most favorable conditions (early-arriving students receive two years of native-language support), English language learners can be expected to test at grade level in English in five to seven years. Under less than favorable conditions (for example, when students have little to no formal education), students might not become proficient for seven to ten years.

In his early work on English language learners, Cummins (1984) described language acquisition as an iceberg. The tip of the iceberg—the small part that is visible above the water—is conversational English, which Cummins described as "basic interpersonal communicative skills," or BICS. This is the language of normal everyday speech, including pronunciation, grammar, and basic vocabulary. It is the ability to understand and speak informally with friends, teachers, and parents. This conversational ability is not especially demanding intellectually, and non-English-speaking children typically can develop it after about two years of living in an English-speaking country.

Because they have developed a conversational ability, these children sound fluent to many people. They understand the teacher's questions, converse with classmates in English, and even translate for their parents. However, their daily schoolwork and exams may not reflect this fluency. Frustrated parents and teachers, faced with this contradiction, often conclude falsely that such students have learning disabilities, are poorly motivated, or are just plain lazy.

If we apply the iceberg metaphor to our fluent but underachieving students, we are likely to see that they have developed only the tip—conversational English. They have not developed academic English—the large portion of the iceberg that is hidden under the sea.

Academic English, which Cummins (1984) describes as cognitive academic language proficiency, or CALP, is the language of the classroom—the language of isosceles triangles, complex compound sentences, and photosynthesis. Students must master academic English to understand textbooks, write papers and reports, solve mathematical word problems, and take tests. Without a mastery of academic English, students cannot develop the critical thinking and problem-solving skills needed to understand and express the new and abstract concepts taught in the classroom. Again, however, academic language takes at least five to seven years to develop, and it can take even longer for students who were not literate in their primary language when they started in a U.S. school (Collier & Thomas, 1989).

Summing Up

When you are familiar with the stages of second-language acquisition, you will be more attuned to the appropriate types of questions and prompts to use to motivate and engage your students in the process of learning English. By understanding your students' levels of linguistic proficiency, you will become more competent at differentiating instruction to promote linguistic and academic achievement.

Understanding the stages of second-language acquisition will help you understand the language applications for each of the nine categories of instructional strategies in the second edition of *Classroom Instruction That Works*. In each of the following chapters, the stages of second-language acquisition provide a lens for examining the language demands of classroom content.

Part I

Creating the Environment
for Learning

3

Setting Objectives and Providing Feedback

Setting objectives in the classroom helps focus the direction for learning and the path for teaching. For students who are learning English, setting objectives is especially important. Imagine the incredible amount of incoming stimuli bombarding these students as they try to learn both a new language *and* content knowledge. This sense of being overwhelmed can subside when students are told exactly what they are going to learn each day upon entering the classroom.

Just as language learning cannot occur if we focus only on subject matter, content knowledge cannot grow if we focus only on language learning. When we set objectives for second-language learners, we need to set both language objectives and content objectives. To do that, we first need to determine the language functions and structures of each lesson.

Setting Objectives: Classroom Practice Recommendations

To set learning objectives in the classroom, the second edition of *Classroom Instruction That Works* provides three recommendations:

- Set learning objectives that are specific but not restrictive.
- Communicate the learning objectives to students and parents.
- Connect the learning objectives to previous and future learning.

Set learning objectives that are specific but not restrictive. The second edition of *Classroom Instruction That Works* instructs us to write learning objectives that are neither too broad (to the point of being meaningless—for example, "Know patterns of power from the Mediterranean to India") or too narrow (in that they limit opportunities for differentiation—for example, "Describe India's caste system in three sentences") but rather just right (for example, "Understand the significance of the caste system in India"). Remember, the learning objective is not an activity (for example, "Read pages 114–117 and answer the questions about the caste system in India").

For English language learners and others in need of language development, however, setting learning objectives is not enough. For example, how likely are your English language learners to have encountered the word *caste*? Because many students acquiring English as another language are in mainstream classrooms for the entire school day, teachers need to support both language and content development (Freeman & Freeman, 2009). To develop language objectives, we will highlight the action of talking, as well as function and structure, with an emphasis on those elements that support the language necessary to meet the content standards. To set language objectives, teachers need to determine the language functions and structures the student needs in order to participate in the lesson, as described in Chapter 1.

Teachers can use a template to determine the language objectives for their lessons. This planning template helps keep the language objective specific enough to allow teachers to take action but not so restrictive that it does not allow for differentiation. Figure 3.1 illustrates a completed template for planning language objectives. (A blank template is available in Appendix C.)

Think about engaging students in setting personal learning objectives, which can help increase their motivation and help them identify how what they're learning is relevant to them (Brophy, 2004). In addition to personalizing content objectives, students can also personalize language objectives by selecting which vocabulary words they would like to learn.

Communicate the learning objectives to students and parents. Clearly communicating learning objectives to students helps them understand and focus on what you want them to learn. Communicating the objectives to parents provides them with an opportunity to engage in and support their children's learning. For students who are culturally and linguistically diverse, we want to communicate not only content objectives but also language objectives.

FIGURE 3.1
Example of a Completed Template for Planning Language Objectives

STEP 1: Determine the Language Functions

Language Function	General Examples	Specific Examples
• What is the purpose for communication in this lesson? • What does the learner have to accomplish with the language?	to name, to describe, to classify, to compare, to explain, to predict, to infer, to suggest, to evaluate, to request	Describe (an animal). Explain (eating habits).

STEP 2: Determine the Language Structures *(Choose 1, 2, or all 3 parts.)*

Language Structure	General Examples	Specific Examples
1. Sentence Starters: What is the phrasing needed? What is an appropriate sentence frame?	• This is a _____. • The ____ lives in _____. • I believe ____ is going to ____ because ____.	• The (animal name) has ___. • The (animal name) is ___. • Although (plural animal name) are ___, they also ____.
2. Key Words: What are some important vocabulary words or terms?	• Content vocabulary for objects, places, measurements, time • Prepositions, adjectives • Connectors (*although*, *as soon as*, *on the day that*)	• Animal body vocabulary, such as *paws, claws, tail, fur, snout, mammal, reptile, bird* • Adjectives for animals, such as *large, bulky, slender, fierce, tranquil*
3. Minilesson: How can you use grammar in an authentic context?	• Command form of verbs • Simple future for prediction • (___ *is going to* + verb) • Word order • Idioms	• Word order with adjectives: The antelope is <u>graceful</u>. The <u>graceful</u> antelope runs. • Idiomatic expressions: *at a snail's pace, busy as a beaver, to be a workhorse.*

Teachers can post both content and language objectives at the front of the room and refer to them throughout the class day. Communicating language and content objectives to parents can take place during parent-teacher conference time, with translators available.

TRY THIS: Incorporate language objectives into your content objectives.

Denver Public Schools in Colorado incorporates language objectives into their content objectives. Here are four examples:
- I will use the transition words *first*, *next*, and *furthermore* while talking about China.
- I will plan and then verbally rehearse before writing an essay.
- I will verbally summarize what I have read.
- I will use the clause starters *before*, *after*, and *while* when retelling what I have read.

Connect the learning objectives to previous and future learning. Although most teachers already naturally connect learning objectives to previous and future learning, it's important to make this explicit. For teachers of emerging English users, this means they will not only connect the content objective to previously learned subject matter but also connect the language objective to previously learned language. Teachers can add on to previously learned content vocabulary and show students the words they have previously learned along with the new vocabulary they will encounter.

Using the Thinking Language Matrix

Figure 3.2 shows how a 4th grade teacher used the Thinking Language Matrix to include all English language learners in the learning objective of making predictions. Mr. Stone's 4th graders are learning to make, confirm, and revise predictions using *Charlie and the Chocolate Factory* by Roald Dahl. Mr. Stone has a number of English language learners and other students in need of language development in his class, and he has decided to engage all of his students in the learning objective by directing them to read a portion of the text and then discuss and predict how Charlie will act next. First, Mr. Stone identifies the taxonomic level of the task—when we ask students to make predictions in the reading process, we're asking them to work at the Application level of

Bloom's taxonomy. They must take what they know (their background knowledge) and apply it to a new situation (what will happen next). Then Mr. Stone thinks about what he expects his proficient students to say: "I predict Charlie is going to taste the forbidden chocolate." Next, he thinks about sentence starters and an element of grammar that his Early Production and Speech Emergence students will need in order to make predictions. Finally, he determines what his Preproduction students can do to function at an Application level.

FIGURE 3.2
Thinking Language Matrix for Making Predictions

Levels of Thinking and Language Functions	Tiered Thinking Across Stages of Second-Language Acquisition				
Level of thinking and academic language required for any task; move from concrete recall to more complex, abstract levels.	Language moves from simple to complex in grammatical tenses, forms, vocabulary, etc.				
	WORD ⟶ MODEL ⟶ EXPAND ⟶ SOUND LIKE A BOOK				
	Preproduction: nonverbal response	**Early Production:** one-word response	**Speech Emergence:** phrases or short sentences	**Intermediate Fluency:** longer and more complex sentences	**Advanced Fluency:** near native
Application apply, choose, demonstrate, dramatize, employ, illustrate, interpret, operate, practice, schedule, sketch, solve, use	Sketch a picture to show what will happen next.	Sentence starter: I predict _____. A minilesson in grammar could focus on ways to express future tense: *is going to* versus *will*.		"I predict Charlie is going to taste the forbidden chocolate."	

Opportunities to develop oral academic language

Teachers of students learning English and other students in need of language development can develop language as well as subject-matter knowledge and skills by providing opportunities for students to engage in meaningful interactions related to specific content, using not just conversational or everyday language but also rich academic language. Well-developed oral academic language proficiency leads to well-developed literacy skills. Supporting rich oral academic language is akin to fostering enhanced comprehension for reading and improved written communication. Figure 3.3 illustrates how to use the Academic Language Framework for teaching both content and language.

FIGURE 3.3
Academic Language Framework for 5th Grade Social Studies

Task	Exemplars	Academic Language			
		Function of Language	Vocabulary	Grammar	Sentence Starter(s)
Compare ancient civilizations.	"Ancient Romans and Mayans are similar because they both grew corn."	comparing	*similar, different, although, based on, as opposed to*	conjunction *because*	Based on _____, the Romans and Mayans are similar because they both _____.

The content objective is to compare ancient civilizations. First, the teacher "goes to the balcony" and looks down on her 5th grade class, seated in small groups to discuss the similarities and differences of the ancient civilizations they're studying. This task is recorded in the Task area of the framework.

Then the teacher predicts what she would like to hear from her most proficient students. For example, "Ancient Romans and Mayans are similar because they both grew corn." This is recorded as an exemplar in the framework.

Next, the teacher begins to identify the academic language by determining the language function—comparing—and recording this in the Function of Language column. Finally, she decides what students acquiring English need in order to engage at the exemplary level of academic talk:

- Vocabulary: *similar, different, although, based on, as opposed to*
- Grammar: using the conjunction *because*
- Sentence starters: *Based on _____, the Romans and Mayans were similar because they both _____.*

By thinking about exemplars, the function of language, and its accompanying vocabulary, grammar, and sentence starters, the teacher can teach both the academic language and the core subject matter.

Providing Feedback: Classroom Practice Recommendations

Effective learning requires feedback. The second edition of *Classroom Instruction That Works* offers four classroom recommendations for providing feedback:

- Provide feedback that addresses what is correct and elaborates on what students need to do next.
- Provide feedback appropriately in time to meet students' needs.
- Provide feedback that is criterion referenced.
- Engage students in the feedback process.

Provide feedback that addresses what is correct and elaborates on what students need to do next. If teachers don't set (and students don't understand) the learning objectives, feedback will have limited utility. When teaching students acquiring English as another language, it is particularly important to ensure that your feedback is comprehensible, useful, and relevant. Oliver (2003) notes that the way in which teachers correct language usage affects students' verbal modifications. When teacher feedback on errors is constructive, students use the feedback to rephrase. According to Schoen and Schoen (2003) and Short (1991), rather than immediately correcting students, teachers should simply restate what the students say using the correct grammar, pronunciation, or vocabulary. Students can refer to this model in the future when they want to say something similar. Modeling correct grammar is beneficial for the student, but overemphasizing grammar is not.

Provide feedback appropriately in time to meet students' needs. The timing of feedback can be critical for second-language learners, particularly when you are offering feedback by verbally modeling correct grammar or pronunciation. For content knowledge, the timing of feedback seems to be contingent on the nature of the learning task. When students are acquiring new, complex knowledge or skills, real-time checks for understanding and guidance can prevent them from developing misconceptions or incorrect practices. By contrast, when they are extending and applying knowledge (for example, writing an essay, designing a science fair project, or solving complex theorems), delayed feedback may be preferable to allow students to self-correct, develop perseverance, and take responsibility for achieving their own learning objectives. For students who are culturally and linguistically diverse, conferencing is our preferred method of feedback, so the cause of any misconceptions or inaccurate practices can be traced, and teacher-student talk can focus on improvement strategies.

Provide feedback that is criterion referenced. The research indicates that using criterion-referenced feedback is more effective than using norm-referenced feedback. In other words, telling students how they are progressing in learning specific types of knowledge and skills is better than giving them a score that reflects the number of correct answers. The practice of using rubrics, a method of providing criterion-referenced feedback, is especially helpful for students acquiring English. Rubrics indicate areas of strength for students learning English, which can be motivating, along with weak areas, which pinpoint the need for revisions and practice.

Engage students in the feedback process. Second-language learners can monitor their own progress in learning English and subject-area content by keeping track of their performance as language and academic learning occur. One way to engage students acquiring English as another language in the feedback process, and to encourage oral language development at the same time, is through reciprocal teaching. Reciprocal teaching is "a form of scaffolded dialogue in which students and teachers construct meaning from text" (Coley & DePinto, 1989, p. 1) and in which responsibility for being the "teacher" gradually becomes the student's.

Teachers can use this strategy with students learning English and others in need of language development to revise written work and cultivate constructive peer feedback through spoken language. For example, a teacher could share and discuss a piece of text using the four reciprocal teaching roles: summarizing, questioning, clarifying, and predicting. After students participate in oral discourse about the text, they write about what they've learned. The opportunity for feedback occurs when students use the four roles to interact with text written by a peer. In small groups, students can summarize what a peer has written, construct questions about the peer's written work, illuminate anything that needs clarification, and predict what might be added. Students can then use the constructive feedback from their peers to revise their written work. Reciprocal teaching makes the connection between oracy and literacy because it gives students the chance to read, talk, and write.

Using the Thinking Language Matrix

The Thinking Language Matrix can be used to include second-language learners at all stages of English language acquisition in the reciprocal teaching activity described in the previous section. We are essentially asking students to evaluate and analyze their peers' work based on a structured conversation.

The example that follows explains how a teacher might go through the process of creating the completed matrix shown in Figure 3.4. The matrix allows the teacher to consider not only the level of thinking of the content he or she is providing students but also what opportunities and supports are available to support students' language development during the activity.

In this example, a 4th grade teacher is working with his students to develop and use descriptive language in writing. He provides students with several descriptions of characters from stories with which they are familiar, and the students identify descriptive language about those characters. Next, the students read a new story that includes several character descriptions. Students select their favorite character in the story to describe in a paragraph using their own words. Feedback on the writing is provided to students through a reciprocal teaching conversation.

The teacher considers the taxonomy level and language demands of the reciprocal teaching roles of summarizer, questioner, and predictor. For example, the questioner might want to ask why the student wrote about a particular character and why that character was the student's favorite. This question appears at the Analysis level of the taxonomy. Beginning with students in the Intermediate and Advanced Fluency stages, the teacher then uses the matrix to anticipate what the student, in the role of questioner, might say. "Why is this character your favorite one? What makes him or her special?" Students at the Early Production and Speech Emergence stages will need the support of sentence starters and perhaps a word bank. Preproduction students will rely on picture and universal hand signals, while still engaging their peers in evaluative "discussion."

FIGURE 3.4

Thinking Language Matrix for 4th Grade Descriptive Language in Writing

Levels of Thinking and Language Functions	Tiered Thinking Across Stages of Second-Language Acquisition				
Level of thinking and academic language required for any task; move from concrete recall to more complex, abstract levels.	Language moves from simple to complex in grammatical tenses, forms, vocabulary, etc.				
	WORD ⟶ MODEL ⟶ EXPAND ⟶ SOUND LIKE A BOOK				
	Preproduction: nonverbal response	**Early Production:** one-word response	**Speech Emergence:** phrases or short sentences	**Intermediate Fluency:** longer and more complex sentences	**Advanced Fluency:** near native
Evaluation appraise, argue, assess, attach, choose, compare, defend, estimate, evaluate, judge, predict, rate, select, support, value	Predictor: Given a drawing of the character described by the writer, the student adds to the picture—colors, facial expressions, clothing, and so on, as suggestions for improvement.	Predictor sentence starter: If you added _____, then your character _____.		Predictor: "If you added more descriptive words to your piece, then the reader would be better able to visualize your character."	
Synthesis arrange, assemble, collect, compose, construct, create, design, develop, formulate, manage, organize, plan, prepare, propose, set up	Summarizer: Using pictures of characters from the story, the student selects the one described by the student writer.	Summarizer sentence starter: Your paragraph tells about _____.		Summarizer: "This paragraph describes a student's favorite character in the story."	
Analysis analyze, appraise, calculate, categorize, compare, contrast, criticize, differentiate, discriminate, distinguish, examine, experiment, question, test	Questioner: Using pictures of characters from the story, the student shows them to the peer writer, who uses thumb up, sideways, or down to show his or her favorite character.	Questioner sentence starter: Why do you like _____ more than _____? OR Why do you like _____ most?		Questioner: "Why is this character your favorite one? What makes him or her special?"	

Opportunities to develop oral academic language

When Jane Hill, one of the authors of this book, was studying Spanish in Mexico and Spain, she knew what she wanted to say. However, when she tried to say it, she ended up in a big "word mess"—entangled in a string of disjointed nouns, verbs, and adjectives. Today, when she works with English language learners on language development, she uses the term *Word-MES* to remind her to

- Provide feedback on **Word** selection with Preproduction students.
- **Model** for Early Production students.
- **Expand** what Speech Emergence students have said.
- Help Intermediate and Advanced Fluency students **"Sound like a book."**

The primary focus of Word-MES is oral language. Whenever you support word choice and model, expand, and help students sound like a book, you are catering to their oral proficiency needs. When you employ the Word-MES strategy, you become conscious of the oral language being used by the student. You have to be a good listener to uncover the *words* needed by a student still learning English. To *model* how something is said correctly in English, you have to be attuned to what a student is saying, so you can hear any errors. To be able to *expand*, you have to be adept at listening to and expanding what students say to include an additional word or a phrase. Finally, to help students *sound like a book*, you need to run oral language through this filter: *Are students using everyday conversational language, and if so, what can I give them to shift their talk to an academic level—the kind of talk found in books and on tests?* For example, let's say that your students are talking about the chronological sequence of a story. Are they using common everyday words such as *next* and *then*? If so, move them into academic language by encouraging the use of words such as *preceding* and *initially*.

Tips for Teaching Using Setting Objectives and Providing Feedback

- To strengthen the indispensable focus on discourse, distinguish between language objectives and those for reading and writing. Language objectives are designed for accountable student talk, and reading and writing objectives are for the content area of literacy.
- Remember that in order to teach the academic language of content, setting language objectives in addition to content objectives is critical. The language objective can be combined into the content objective. For example, this objective for writing contains a verbal component as well: "Students will write a persuasive essay draft by first verbally sharing their opinions and two or three supporting facts using the sentence starters 'I think . . .' or 'In my opinion, . . .'
- Because students in the process of learning English need to learn language alongside content, identify the vocabulary and syntax they will need in order to participate in academic discourse with the rest of the class.
- Setting language objectives should not involve vocabulary alone; vocabulary is just the tip of the iceberg. When planning for language objectives, think of what elements of grammar can accompany the subject-matter learning.
- In addition to building language objectives for vocabulary and grammar, set objectives for discourse. Pauline Gibbons (2006) says that discourse strategies are used by a teacher to facilitate accountable talk. Therefore, teachers should be PIE (purposeful, intentional, and explicit) in planning for academic talk.
- When providing feedback, write the term *Word-MES* in your lesson plans to remind yourself to use this feedback strategy.
- Two things English language learners really want to know are "Will the teacher like me?" and "Can I do the work?" Providing feedback on English acquisition will demonstrate an aspect of "like" they may not have experienced before.

- Errors are naturally going to occur in the process of learning a second language, and the best way for you, as a teacher, to deal with them is to model correct structures by unceremoniously restating what students say. Overtly correcting grammar and pronunciation can generate anxiety, which in turn can inhibit normal language acquisition.

4

Reinforcing Effort and Providing Recognition

Reinforcing effort enhances students' understanding of the relationship between effort and achievement by addressing their attitudes and beliefs about learning. You'll find that students attribute success to different causes: ability, effort, other people, and luck. Ask a group of young students who among them is the best soccer player and why, and they will likely say, "She's just good at everything," "She's a natural athlete," or "It runs in her family. Her older sister's an all-star." Ask the soccer player herself what makes her so good and she will say, "Practicing every day after school," "Exercising to increase strength and agility," or "Attending summer soccer camp"—in other words, *effort*.

Reinforcing Effort: Classroom Practice Recommendations

Because not all students recognize the importance of believing in effort, teachers must understand the relationship between effort and achievement and expose students to the connection between the two. The second edition of *Classroom Instruction That Works* provides three classroom practice recommendations for reinforcing effort:

- Teach students about the relationship between effort and achievement.
- Provide students with explicit guidance about exactly what it means to expend effort.
- Ask students to keep track of their effort and achievement.

  Teach students about the relationship between effort and achievement. This recommendation will benefit students learning English and native

English-speaking students alike, but English language learners are doing double duty: learning new content in a new language. Teaching students about the relationship between effort and achievement involves telling them personal stories from your own life about times when effort led to success. You can also provide students with examples from the lives of well-known people such as sports stars, historical figures, and political leaders. If it is an Olympic year, remind students to pay attention to the "up-close and personal" stories of the athletes, which are loaded with examples of effort leading to achievement.

Example

Linking Effort to Achievement
Grade Level: Any
Strategy: Teach the correlation between effort and achievement.

To teach her English language learners the correlation between effort and achievement, a Colorado high school teacher showed her students part of Lindsey Vonn's news conference after winning the gold medal in the downhill event at the Vancouver 2010 Winter Olympics. At the gathering, Ms. Vonn said, "I've been working for this my whole life." The teacher explained to her students that hard work is equated with achievement, and she provided other examples as well.

Provide students with explicit guidance about exactly what it means to expend effort. Students may not always be clear about what it means to expend effort on a task. Let's examine how guidance on expending effort should take place for second-language learners. When teachers conference with students who are acquiring English, they need to be as clear and succinct as possible in explaining what a product should look like and how to reach an end result based on the student's stage of second-language acquisition. Note that if English language learners are expected to accomplish the exact same product as non–English language learners, then they will not understand the effort-achievement connection. This conferencing time will help build the critical relationship and bond between teacher and student. Conferencing time allows teachers to ensure a high level of student engagement with authentic language describing effort—which is particularly important because effort can be a challenging concept for any student to understand.

Example

Adjusting Assignments Based on Stage of Second Language Acquisition
Grade Level: 6
Strategy: Support Preproduction students in creating an alternative to a written report.

Near the end of a unit about the Lewis and Clark expedition, a teacher asks her 6th graders to write a report on the expedition and how the explorers interacted with Native Americans. If culturally and linguistically diverse students are expected to produce the same product, they could put the highest amount of effort possible into the assignment but not achieve what the teacher expects. In this instance, the teacher meets with the Preproduction students and explains that their product will be to arrange 20 photos along a timeline with dates and years that show the route of Lewis and Clark's exploration. Their effort involves looking back at the text and pictures, reviewing online resources provided by the teacher, and asking questions when they're unsure about the content or task.

Figure 4.1 illustrates how we might use a rubric to gauge effort with non–English language learners and also make it suitable for English language learners by reducing the linguistic complexity and adding pictures. When we add pictures as metaphors for difficulty in an effort rubric, we need to align the levels with something familiar. For example, in Figure 4.1, an ice cream sundae is the metaphor for effort: Level 1 is a bowl and spoon; Level 2 shows a scoop of ice cream added; Level 3 adds some chocolate sauce; and Level 4 is the completed dessert with strawberries, whipped cream, and a paper umbrella.

FIGURE 4.1
Effort Rubrics for Non–English Language Learners and English Language Learners

Non–English Language Learner	English Language Learner	
I worked on the task until it was completed. I pushed myself to continue working on the task even when difficulties arose or a solution was not immediately evident. I viewed difficulties that arose as opportunities to strengthen my understanding.		I worked until I finished. I tried even when it was difficult. This lesson helped me learn more English.
I worked on the task until it was completed. I pushed myself to continue working on the task even when difficulties arose or a solution was not immediately evident.		I worked until I finished. I tried even when it was difficult.
I put some effort into the task, but I stopped working when difficulties arose.		I tried, but I stopped when it was too difficult.
I put very little effort into the task.		I didn't try.

Students acquiring English who are not familiar with American culture will need a teacher's direct guidance on expending effort. They will need exemplars based on their respective stage of second-language acquisition and advice on how to pay attention, make connections to what they already know, and

---

FIGURE 4.2
Example of an Effort Checklist for Summarizing

□ 4 = I thought about what the text reminded me of.
- I asked questions.
- I searched for the main idea.
- I looked for supporting details and evidence to support the main idea.
- I predicted what would happen next.
- I made a movie in my mind about what I was reading.

□ 3 = I thought about what the text reminded me of.
- I asked questions.
- I tried to find the main idea and supporting evidence.

□ 2 = I asked many questions.

□ 1 = I made something up.

---

seek clarification. With the teacher's help, they can develop an effort checklist for an assignment, with a 1-to-4 rating scale, such as the example in Figure 4.2.

Ask students to keep track of their effort and achievement. Helping students who are acquiring English as another language track effort and achievement also provides an opportunity for language facilitation. Teachers can act as language facilitators by providing students with models for how to talk about effort and achievement, using think-alouds and sentence starters.

In addition to understanding and creating their own effort rubrics, emerging English users will need conferencing on the achievement rubric the teacher will use. What do the teacher's scores of 1, 2, 3, and 4 mean? For example, a 7th grade math teacher wants students to work in pairs to determine the new area and perimeter of a shape when one of its dimensions is doubled in length. The achievement rubric he will use is shown in Figure 4.3. Students who are acquiring English can practice their oral language development by talking about what it means to put forth effort sufficient to reach a 3 or 4 level of attainment.

FIGURE 4.3
Example of an Achievement Rubric

4 Advanced	3 Proficient	2 Partially Proficient	1 Novice
Explain and provide supporting examples of how measurements of common shapes are affected when one of the attributes is changed in some way.	Determine how measurements of common shapes are affected when one of the attributes is changed in some way, with no significant errors.	Determine how measurements of common shapes are affected when one of the attributes is changed in some way, with a few significant errors.	Determine how measurements of common shapes are affected when one of the attributes is changed in some way, with many significant errors.

We can combine an effort rubric and an achievement rubric to help students track the relationship between effort and achievement (see Figure 4.4). The student will be prompted to make connections. For example, the student put some effort into the homework assignment for October 22 but stopped when it became difficult. On October 26, the student said, "I worked until I finished. I tried even when it was difficult. This lesson helped me learn more English." As a result, the student received a 3 (Proficient) rather than the 1 recorded on October 22.

FIGURE 4.4
Rubric for Tracking Effort and Achievement

Name:

Date	Assignment/Activity/Lesson	Effort Rubric	Achievement Rubric
Oct. 22	Homework	2	1
Oct. 26	Quiz	4	3
Oct. 31	Assignment	4	4
Nov. 1	Assignment	2	2

TRY THIS: Introduce students to effort and achievement rubrics.

A high school social studies teacher in Colorado reported that he was "amazed" by the difference the effort and achievement tracking system made for his students, many of whom were English language learners. He established a rubric for effort and explained it with think-alouds and examples. An achievement rubric was already in place, and when he linked the two rubrics together, his students began to see the connections between effort and achievement, and they were motivated to match their effort to their performance.

Using the Thinking Language Matrix

The Thinking Language Matrix can be used to include students at all stages of English language acquisition in reinforcing effort. When we ask students to compare their effort to their achievement, we are asking them to analyze their performance. Here's the process a teacher might go through to create the completed matrix shown in Figure 4.5.

An algebra teacher is conferencing with his students to support them in making a connection between their achievement on tests and the amount of time and effort they put into studying for those tests. He visualizes a conference with a fluent English speaker who might say, "When I studied for at least an hour, I got an *A* on my algebra test. When I forgot to study, my grade went down." Taking a short time to show Early Production and Speech Emergent students the structure of the sentence—and providing them with a sentence starter—will result in a conversation similar to the one the teacher has with the fluent students, at the same high level of thinking. The Preproduction students can also participate through picture metaphors that represent levels of effort, which can then be aligned with test grades.

FIGURE 4.5
Thinking Language Matrix for Relationship Between Effort and Achievement

Levels of Thinking and Language Functions	Tiered Thinking Across Stages of Second-Language Acquisition				
Level of thinking and academic language required for any task; move from concrete recall to more complex, abstract levels.	Language moves from simple to complex in grammatical tenses, forms, vocabulary, etc.				
	WORD ⟶ MODEL ⟶ EXPAND ⟶ SOUND LIKE A BOOK				
	Preproduction: nonverbal response	**Early Production:** one-word response	**Speech Emergence:** phrases or short sentences	**Intermediate Fluency:** longer and more complex sentences	**Advanced Fluency:** near native
Analysis analyze, appraise, calculate, categorize, compare, contrast, criticize, differentiate, discriminate, distinguish, examine, experiment, question, test	The student creates a series of pictures using the same theme, which represent degrees of effort. She writes the grade for each algebra test taken and draws the picture that best represents her effort when studying for the test.		A minilesson in grammar could focus on using a dependent clause starting with when. Sentence starter: When I _____, then _____.	"When I studied for at least an hour, then I got an A on my algebra test. When I forgot to study, then my grade went down."	

Opportunities to develop oral academic language

Whole-class, small-group, and teacher-to-student conversations all provide opportunities for students to practice using oral academic language while making connections to effort. What did students have to do to improve their English language learning and content learning? You might ask students to develop their own checklist of the effort needed for learning English, which can strengthen their language learning and be applied to the tracking of their own effort and achievement.

Consider asking second-language learners to share their language-learning experiences with other students. Native English-speaking students may not have any conception of what it takes to learn a second language.

Providing Recognition: Classroom Practice Recommendations

When we provide recognition, we acknowledge students' attainment of their goals (Dean et al., 2012). The research on providing recognition is mixed; some research, for example, suggests that praise can negatively impact students' intrinsic motivation (e.g., Henderlong & Lepper, 2002; Kamins & Dweck, 1999), whereas other research notes that recognition can positively impact student engagement and behavior when it focuses on students' individual mastery of a task rather than compares them to others (Moore-Partin, Robertson, Maggin, Oliver, & Wehby, 2012). The second edition of *Classroom Instruction That Works* provides the following recommendations for providing recognition:

- Promote a mastery-goal orientation.
- Provide praise that is specific and aligned with expected performance and behaviors.
- Use concrete symbols of recognition.

Promote a mastery-goal orientation. Mastery-goal orientations emphasize learning and meeting goals rather than comparing students' performances (Dean et al., 2012). This approach can be particularly useful when teaching students who are in the process of acquiring English, as it provides an opportunity for teachers not only to differentiate goals for students but also to provide personal recognition for students when they meet those goals. When we promote a mastery-goal orientation, students know what they need to do to succeed, because teachers have defined the effort needed to achieve the goal. If students are not successful, then they can reevaluate their effort and achievement to decide what else they can do to meet the target. Students should be reinforced for achieving the goal rather than have their performances rated relative to other students.

For example, a high school teacher wanted to increase the focus on learning in her classroom and decrease attention to students' relative ability levels. To emphasize this learning orientation, the teacher explained the content objectives and helped students personalize their learning goals. The teacher knew that students would be more engaged when they were given tasks that connected to their background knowledge and interests. Each student had individualized learning goals and expectations. However, when the teacher thought she had laid the necessary groundwork for promoting a mastery-goal orientation, something happened that she didn't anticipate: the English language learners didn't seem interested in their individualized plans.

The teacher noticed that students who are learning English were always talking with one another rather than asking her questions directly. She discovered something interesting about her students: they had a cultural obligation to help one another. As high schoolers learning new content in a new language in a far-from-home environment, they were honor-bound to stick together, help one another decipher assignments, and figure out new and puzzling school rules. This contradicted what she knew was important to highly competitive American students who want to be the best in the class. Because her students acquiring English were from cultures that respect cooperation and group values, she relaxed her emphasis on individual student work and initiated small-group cooperative learning pursuits.

Provide praise that is specific and aligned with expected performance and behaviors. An example of this recommendation is providing recognition when a culturally and linguistically diverse student moves from one stage of language proficiency to the next.

Example

> **Praise and Recognition**
> **Grade Level:** Any
> **Strategy:** Offer specific praise aligned to objectives.

Mr. Brown is a middle school English as a Second Language teacher. He uses the WIDA (World-Class Instructional Design and Assessment) ACCESS for ELLs (Assessing Comprehension and Communication in English State-to-State for English Language Learners), with its six levels: 1—Entering; 2—Beginning; 3—Developing; 4—Expanding; 5—Bridging; 6—Reaching. Whenever his Level 1 (Entering) students move to the next level, 2 (Beginning), he praises their achievement. He continues to praise students as they pass from one level of language gain to the next. Praise is also provided when a student has reached the English proficiency level needed to exit the English language learner program, because it focuses on the attainment of an established goal.

In addition to knowing the expectation for moving through the stages of English language proficiency, we need to be aware of how a culture might influence students' responses to praise and recognition (see Figure 4.6). If we are only aware of the "tip of the iceberg" (that is, general information about such things as food, dress, and language), then we may miss opportunities to be culturally sensitive when providing recognition. For example, Hispanic culture places a high priority on family. Therefore, if we are setting up an awards ceremony involving Hispanic students, it will be more meaningful for these students if their families are present at the ceremony. Looking again "below the water line," we see a "concept of cleanliness." In some Middle Eastern and Asian cultures, it is impolite to give or receive items with the left hand. Therefore, we may need to rethink the practice of shaking a person's right hand while giving an award (or a diploma!) with the left hand. Being aware of other unspoken rules will make us pay attention to types of food we use at a recognition party. For example, Muslims must avoid pork products, which are sometimes found in snack foods, such as chips, crackers, and cookies, in the form of lard.

Use concrete symbols of recognition. In addition to verbal acknowledgment, teachers can give students concrete symbols of recognition, such as awards, certificates, or coupons. These can be given for attaining a certain performance goal but should not be provided simply for completing a task or be offered as rewards per se. Different students might enjoy different kinds of tokens. For students acquiring English as another language, a happy-face sticker can have more meaning than a written comment.

Here, again, other cultural considerations may need to come into play. For example, when using concrete symbols for recognition on paper, you might want to avoid red ink, which has negative connotations for some Korean, Mexican, and Chinese families (Dresser, 1996).

FIGURE 4.6
The Iceberg Concept of Culture

Like an iceberg, nine-tenths of culture is below the surface

food • dress • visual arts • drama • crafts • dance • literature • language • celebrations • games

Surface Culture
Above sea level
Emotional load relatively low

Unspoken Rules
Partially below sea level
Emotional load very high

Unconscious Rules
Completely below sea level
Emotional load intense

courtesy • contextual conversational patterns • concept of time • personal space • rules of conduct • facial expressions • nonverbal communication • body language • touching • eye contact • patterns of handling emotions • notions of modesty • concept of beauty • courtship practices • relationships to animals • notions of leadership • tempo of work • concepts of food • ideas of childrearing • theory of disease • social interaction rate • nature of friendships • tone of voice • attitudes toward elders • concept of cleanliness • notions of adolescence • patterns of group decision-making • definition of insanity • preference for competition or cooperation • tolerance of physical pain • concept of "self" • concept of past and future • definition of obscenity • attitudes toward dependents • problem-solving • roles in relation to age, sex class, occupation, kinship, and so forth

Source: Indiana Department of Education, Division of Language Minority and Migrant Programs

Example

> **Differentiated Rewards**
> **Grade Level:** Elementary
> **Strategy:** Provide rewards aligned with student preferences.

Miss Watson is a K–6 teacher of English as a Second Language. When her students move from one WIDA level to the next, she differentiates her tangible rewards based on individual student interests. She asks each of her English language learners what they would like as a concrete reward when they advance to the next WIDA level. Some students select a toy from her "treasure box," whereas others want a reward certificate to show their parents. Miss Watson finds that her students are attuned to their learning of English and want to know their results as soon as possible. She favors this strategy because in the past, she did not share the WIDA results with students; the scores were only used by her school's data team.

Tips for Teaching Using Reinforcing Effort and Providing Recognition

- Remember that although not all students will realize the importance of believing in effort, you can teach them that effort is related to achievement. The belief in effort will serve as a powerful motivational tool that students can apply in any class or situation. Emerging English users will need additional opportunities to discuss the linkages between effort and achievement.
- In addition to structuring talk time around effort and achievement, become an effort-achievement advocate by building concrete examples into the curriculum.
- Consider the iceberg concept of culture. What do you know about your students' cultures? If you are only aware of the tip of the iceberg (food, dress, crafts, games, language), then you may miss opportunities to be culturally sensitive when providing recognition.

- Be aware of what is important in each student's culture. For example, in Hispanic culture, family is significant, so an awards ceremony in front of the whole school may not be as valuable as one that is part of a family night at school.

5

Cooperative Learning

Mainstream teachers with both English language learners and native English-speaking students in their classrooms can use cooperative learning strategies as a powerful tool for fostering language acquisition. As Dean and her colleagues (2012) note, "Using cooperative learning helps teachers lay the foundation for student success in a world that depends on collaboration and cooperation" (p. 35). According to most writers, there are a number of elements that set cooperative learning apart from other techniques (Cochran, 1989; Johnson & Johnson, 1999). These elements include the following:

- Heterogeneous grouping (combining English language learners and non–English language learners in the same group)
- Positive interdependence (sinking or swimming together)
- Face-to-face supportive interaction (helping one another learn and applauding one another's successes and efforts)
- Individual accountability (requiring each group member to contribute to the group's achievement of its goals; typically, each member is assigned a specific role to perform in the group)
- Interpersonal and small-group skills (communication, trust, leadership, decision making, and conflict resolution)
- Group processing (reflecting on how well the team is functioning and how it can function even better)

Cooperative learning groups have the potential to foster language acquisition in ways that whole-class instruction cannot. So what is it about these groups that makes them such a rich opportunity for students learning English?

Second-language learners working in small groups or with partners have many more opportunities to speak than they do during whole-class instruction. Small groups "create opportunities for sustained dialogue and substantive language use" as students use language to accomplish the task at hand (Zehler, 1994, p. 7). When an art teacher asks the class, "What makes this picture surreal?" and calls on a single student to answer the question, only one student is engaged. When students are directed to discuss with their partners what makes the picture surreal, all students are participating. In fact, cooperative learning groups "demand speech" because each member must carry out his or her role if the group as a whole is to succeed (Alanis, 2004).

Cooperative Learning: Classroom Practice Recommendations

The second edition of *Classroom Instruction That Works* offers three recommendations for cooperative learning classroom practice:

- Include elements of both positive interdependence and individual accountability.
- Keep group size small.
- Use cooperative learning consistently and systematically.

Include elements of both positive interdependence and individual accountability. Positive interdependence means that everyone is indispensable for a group's success. Each member of a small group must recognize that his or her own effort is not only required but also mandatory and that all students "sink or swim" together (Johnson, Johnson, & Holubec, 1998). The element of individual accountability means that although students are learning together as a small group, they are also working alone at times to represent the group. This component is designed to prevent students from "hitchhiking" off the work of others.

Many students in the process of acquiring English may come from classroom environments outside the United States that require students to sit in rows and raise their hands before speaking, and they are not familiar with the way cooperative learning works. When teachers adapt this recommendation for use with culturally and linguistically diverse students, they may need to build the culture for cooperative learning and explain, model, and practice the two elements of positive interdependence and individual accountability before expecting to see them demonstrated in their classrooms by all students.

Example

Modeling Cooperative Learning
Grade Level: Any
Strategy: Build positive interdependence.

The following example illustrates how a teacher can build an element of positive interdependence in the classroom before including it in cooperative learning activities.

Explain: Take students acquiring English as another language to the cafeteria to observe how each person on the cafeteria staff is an integral part of a team. Without each cafeteria worker performing his or her necessary role, students would not receive their lunches. If the cashier were not at the front of the line to collect money or scan cards, students would not be able to pick up their trays. If the dishwashers did not do their jobs, trays would not be available. If the food server were not present, who would dish up portions?

Model: Arrange for a situation in the classroom in which positive interdependence is taking place (for example, assembling a class-made book for everyone to take home to read). Suddenly, you are called away to the door. Does the project grind to a halt?

Practice: Ask students to name environments in which they know everyone must depend on one another to get the job done. Select one example—let's say it's working at a fast-food restaurant—and have the students role-play the various workers who depend on one another to get the orders out to the customers. After the students role-play the operation, one worker is removed and the group discusses the consequences of that worker's absence.

Repeat the same process for developing the component of individual accountability, again using a familiar situation before using it in an academic situation. The goal is to make connections to students' background knowledge. If they can understand individual accountability and what it looks like in their own lives, then they will be better able to demonstrate that component during cooperative learning time in the classroom.

Group members must also "negotiate meaning" as they speak; that is, they must adjust their language so that it is comprehensible to other members. In doing this, students ensure that all members are able to understand what others have said (Englander, 2002; Kagan, 1995).

Keep group size small. Keeping group size small makes sense for all students, but this is particularly true for students acquiring English, who will feel more comfortable speaking in their new language in the confines of a small group of peers. Keeping groups small also increases talk time for second-language learners because they won't have to compete to be heard over a larger number of students. When students are in small groups, it is also easy to check for understanding and adjust the level of speech appropriately—something that a teacher or a student cannot easily do in a whole-class session (Kagan, 1995).

Small groups offer the following additional advantages:

- They allow for the repetition of key words and phrases. For example, when students are talking in small groups or pairs to determine a common denominator, second-language learners hear the term *common denominator* used by others, and they gain practice using the term as they say, for example, "I think the common denominator is 2." According to Kagan (1995), "Language acquisition is not ensured unless input is received repeatedly from a variety of sources" (p. 56). Repetition allows emerging English users not only to comprehend the language in the short term but also to acquire it in the long term (Kagan, 1995).

- They require functional, context-relevant speech. Speech that is personally relevant and related to real-life situations is more likely to add to an English language learner's fluency (Kagan, 1995).
- They are "feedback-rich." There are far more opportunities for feedback and correction in a small-group setting, and that feedback and correction occur in the context of actual conversations rather than in a formal instructional situation. An English language learner is less likely to feel self-conscious about being corrected in a small-group setting (Kagan, 1995).
- They can greatly reduce student anxiety. Because small groups are supportive and interdependent, students in the process of learning English feel more comfortable speaking.

Example

Fostering Group Discussion
Grade Level: Any
Strategy: Encourage English language learners' participation in class.

Mr. Smiley, a middle school language arts teacher, notices that after he poses a question to the class, his second-language-acquisition students never raise their hands. For example, when he asks a question regarding a character's personality traits in a piece of text the whole class has read, the native English speakers all raise their hands to answer, but the English language learners do not. He ponders this dilemma while waiting for a staff meeting to begin. During the meeting, when the principal asks a question of the whole group, he does not raise his hand. It's not that he doesn't know the answer; it's just that he is a first-year teacher and doesn't want to offer an opinion just yet. The principal then breaks the faculty into small groups to discuss the issue. Now Mr. Smiley feels more comfortable expressing his thoughts—and he realizes that the situation could also apply to his students. Taking his personal experience back to his classroom, rather than ask questions of the whole class, Mr. Smiley poses questions for small-group discussion and discovers that his English language learners participate more readily.

Use cooperative learning consistently and systematically. Johnson and Johnson (2009) define three different types of groupings for cooperative learning: formal (lasting several days to complete an assignment), base (lasting for a semester or a year to support students), and informal (talking with students nearby). All three are useful, but the third type can be particularly important for English language learners. Implementing informal cooperative groups will help ensure accountable student talk time. That is, teachers can purposefully plan and assist students in thinking and expressing their reasoning using academic language. Planning and facilitating accountable talk does not mean giving students time to talk for talking's sake. It does mean providing structures for the talk and expectations for the use of specific terminology or forms of grammar. For example, if students are going to be discussing a science concept they just read about, the teacher can set up partners to paraphrase what they understood, using the terms *generally*, *is characterized by*, and *refers to*.

To develop language growth in addition to content learning, students must be given time to talk with one another about the learning taking place. As Jeff Wilhelm (2001) notes, "learning floats on a sea of talk and . . . we must get students to talk through their content understandings and thinking processes" (p. 116). To make this happen, teachers will have to purposefully plan for informal cooperative learning. Figure 5.1 suggests some informal cooperative learning activities.

Discovering a variety of cooperative learning constructs will allow teachers to build a complete toolkit for engaging students in accountable talk. Lesson planning should include multiple opportunities to engage with students. Consider allowing students to talk as much as, if not more than, the teacher. To make accountable talk time happen, it has to be an integral part of daily lesson plans.

FIGURE 5.1
Examples of Informal Cooperative Learning Activities

Activity	Description
Numbered Heads Together (adapted from Kagan, 1992)	The teacher asks a question, and students (each identified by a different number) in a group consult to make sure everyone knows the answer. One student number is called on to answer. 1. Number off the students in each group, up to four. If one group is smaller than the others, ask Student 3 to answer for Student 4 as well. The teacher can assign numbers or students can assign numbers to themselves. 2. Ask students a question or propose a problem to solve. Everyone in the group must be able to participate and answer the question. Ensure that enough wait time is given for the group to do the task. 3. Call out a number, such as 2, and ask each Student 2 to give the answer. This structure ensures that each student is prepared with a response.
Three-Step Interview (adapted from Kagan, 1992)	The teacher seats students in groups of four. Students interview each other in pairs. Students share the information they learned in the interview with the group. 1. Students interview their partners by asking clarifying questions (what, how, when, where, why) about their understanding of a topic, skill, or process. 2. Partners reverse the roles. 3. Students share their partner's responses with the group. This process activates prior knowledge, encourages peer tutoring, and guarantees student talk time. It can also be used to review and reinforce previously learned material.
Three-Minute Review (adapted from Kagan, 1992)	The teacher stops any time during a lecture or discussion and gives groups three minutes to review what has been said, to ask clarifying questions, or to answer questions.
Four Corners (adapted from Himmele & Himmele, 2011)	1. Give students a prompt that requires them to form an opinion. 2. Use Likert-scale options such as Strongly Agree, Agree, Disagree, and Strongly Disagree. 3. Ask students to determine their level of agreement with the prompt and do a Quick-Write expressing their opinion, including reasons why they chose their point of view. 4. Post the response options in four corners of the room. 5. Students walk to the area where their Likert-scale choice is posted. In these groups, students discuss their reasons for choosing the option they did. 6. Each group then reports out to the class. As a follow-up, the teacher can ask students to go to another corner and argue the prompt from that point of view.

Paraphrase Passport (adapted from Kagan, 1992)	Students engaging in group discussion paraphrase what others have said. Before a student can offer an opinion or other input, he or she must paraphrase what was last said.
	The person whose statement was paraphrased indicates whether the speaker has correctly captured the meaning. Once the speaker is satisfied that his or her statement has been accurately paraphrased, the discussion continues with the next speaker's comments.
Inside-Outside Circle (adapted from Kagan, 1992)	Students stand in pairs in two concentric circles. The inside circle faces out; the outside circle faces in. Students respond to the teacher's questions, rotating after each one to a new partner.
	By the end of this activity, students will have been both teachers and learners of new information. This structure also facilitates peer tutoring and checking for different levels of knowledge acquisition.

Using the Thinking Language Matrix

The Thinking Language Matrix can be used to include students at all stages of English language acquisition in a Four Corners activity such as the one described in the next paragraph. The activity, which actually asks students to argue and defend their points of view on a particular issue, falls into the Evaluation level of Bloom's taxonomy. Figure 5.2 shows how the teacher completed the Thinking Language Matrix as part of her planning of the Four Corners activity.

Using a modified Four Corners activity to express and defend opinions is a complex process that might best be practiced first using a familiar context, particularly when working with English language learners. In this case, a 3rd grade teacher decided to use Michael Phelps's historic achievement at the Beijing 2008 Summer Olympics—winning eight gold medals in swimming. She used Phelps's success as an example of effort leading to achievement and as a way to teach a modified version of the Four Corners structure. Rather than using a Likert scale (Strongly Agree, Agree, Disagree, Strongly Disagree), which is customary in the Four Corners activity, the teacher asked students to choose what they thought was the main reason Phelps was so successful: Other People, Natural Talent, Effort/Practice, or Luck. Each corner represented one of these reasons. Rather than asking for a Quick-Write, the teacher asked students to brainstorm ideas that might fit into each category, and she wrote the ideas on the board. Next, the teacher asked students to stand in the corner that represented their thinking about the main reason for Phelps's success and discuss

FIGURE 5.2
Thinking Language Matrix for a Modified Four Corners Activity

Levels of Thinking and Language Functions	Tiered Thinking Across Stages of Second-Language Acquisition				
Level of thinking and academic language required for any task; move from concrete recall to more complex, abstract levels.	Language moves from simple to complex in grammatical tenses, forms, vocabulary, etc.				
	WORD ⟶ MODEL ⟶ EXPAND ⟶ SOUND LIKE A BOOK				
	Preproduction: nonverbal response	**Early Production:** one-word response	**Speech Emergence:** phrases or short sentences	**Intermediate Fluency:** longer and more complex sentences	**Advanced Fluency:** near native
Evaluation appraise, argue, assess, attach, choose, compare, defend, estimate, evaluate, judge, predict, rate, select, support, value	As reasons are generated during a brainstorm, the teacher or another student creates a nonlinguistic representation (picture) that explains the reason. Students use the pictures to choose the corner where they will stand.	Sentence starter: In my opinion, Phelps won all of those medals because _____. Students select a reason from those brainstormed by the class at the beginning of this activity.		"In my opinion, Phelps won all of those medals because his mother got him out of bed and took him to practice every day."	

TRY THIS: Encourage accountable productive talk.

Before expecting students to engage in the accountable productive talk you are envisaging, give them five minutes to talk about whatever they want to talk about. After this period of free talk, require them to stay on topic and follow the criteria set forth by the informal cooperative learning structure.

that thinking first with others standing in the same corner and then with students standing in other corners.

If the teacher had asked the whole class "What is the main reason for Phelps's success?" and then called on one student, she would have seen limited engagement, particularly from students in the process of learning English, who can be anxious about speaking in front of the whole class. The teacher intentionally used the Four Corners structure to create maximum engagement among all students, and the Thinking Language Matrix provided an additional structure to guide the process for English language learners.

Opportunities to develop oral academic language

Since the launch of high-stakes testing, the urgency around being able to read and write has overshadowed the need for students acquiring English to listen and talk. Even pull-out programs for English as a second language students emphasize reading and writing more than listening and speaking. In addition, once second-language acquisition students reach an intermediate proficiency level and beyond, most of their time in mainstream classrooms is packed with reading and writing pursuits rather than talk time. Native English speakers used to have opportunities to polish their speaking abilities during "show and tell" and in the "dress-up" centers in kindergarten. Recent observations in kindergarten classrooms in the Midwest revealed an elimination of these activities in favor of literacy activities. Because native English speakers are expected to be proficient in reading and writing by 3rd grade, most learning takes place through print and text—not through talking with other students. In teacher-directed classrooms, teachers talk more than students.

What all this means is that if teachers do not plan for oral interaction, it will not happen. When the informal structures described earlier are planned and delivered, the likelihood of communication and collaboration increases. Talking for talking's sake is not the goal, but practice, use, and reinforcement of rich oral academic language should be the expected outcome.

Example

A 3rd grade teacher who wants to intentionally develop students' oral academic language during a math lesson uses an informal cooperative learning structure called Mix-Freeze-Pair (Kagan, 1995). Students stroll around the classroom holding various three-dimensional shapes and not talking. When the teacher calls "freeze," all of the students stop in their tracks. When the teacher says "pair," students talk about the solid shapes and their attributes with the nearest person. The teacher has been intentional in planning for academic talk and explicit by expecting students to sound like a book by using terminology such as *faces*, *vertices*, and *edges*.

In the Common Core State Standards for mathematics, students are expected to make sense of problems and communicate about procedures related to problem solving. To be successful in fostering the rich oral academic language needed for this kind of communication, teachers can use the Academic Language Framework described in Chapter 1. The completed framework in Figure 5.3 shows the teacher's thinking in the 3rd grade math example. The teacher "went to the balcony" to get a big-picture look at the class when students were reasoning about shapes and their attributes. The teacher visualized a task: students describing attributes of solid shapes (such as triangular prisms, rectangular prisms, cones, cylinders, pyramids, and spheres). While still on the balcony, the teacher thought about what his most proficient students would say and used that as an exemplar: "This solid is a triangular prism because it has two bases that are parallel to each other and are classified as triangles. It also has five faces, six vertices, and nine edges." Now that this teacher could visualize students talking in small groups and what they might be saying, he identified the reason—the purpose

FIGURE 5.3
Academic Language Framework for a 3rd Grade Math Lesson

Task	Exemplars	Academic Language			
		Function of Language	**Vocabulary**	**Grammar**	**Sentence Starter(s)**
Describe attributes of solid shapes (e.g., triangular prisms, rectangular prisms, cones, cylinders, pyramids, spheres).	"This solid is a triangular prism because it has two bases that are parallel to each other and are classified as triangles. It also has five faces, six vertices, and nine edges."	describing	*solid, triangular, prism, base, parallel, faces, vertices, edges*	nouns adjectives (how many, how much)	A triangular prism has ___ faces, ___ vertices, and ___ edges.

(function of language)—for the student talk: describing. Next, the teacher thought about what English language learners would need in order to engage in the level of talk associated with the exemplar. There is key vocabulary: *solid, triangular, prism, base, parallel, faces, vertices, edges*. Students acquiring English would also need adjectives (grammar) and sentence starters such as "A triangular prism has ___ faces, ___ vertices, and ___ edges."

Tips for Teaching Using Cooperative Learning

- Strategically plan for where and when to insert structures for cooperative learning, because they might not occur naturally. With practice, you will begin to intuitively use the structures.
- Strive to include all students at all stages of language acquisition by creatively adapting cooperative learning structures so that everyone—limited-English-proficient and fluent students alike—can practice the language of content. The example about Michael Phelps exemplifies full and simultaneous inclusion of all students at all stages of second-language acquisition.

- Include reciprocal teaching (see Chapter 8) in your repertoire of cooperative learning structures; it works well for comprehending text and for providing feedback on writing.
- Remember that cooperative learning structures may increase student motivation because they include the movement and interaction many students require.

Part II

Helping Students Develop Understanding

6

Cues, Questions, and Advance Organizers

Students construct meaning by drawing connections between new information and what they already know—their background knowledge. As a strategy, cueing and questioning is responsible for a full 80 percent of teacher-student interactions (Fillippone, 1998), and it's not hard to see why. Cueing and questioning activates students' background knowledge, helps them determine what they don't yet know, and provides hints about what's coming next, all of which help students construct meaning around the content.

We all interpret information based on our prior experiences, or schema, and English-language-learning students are likely to enter the classroom with schema that are markedly different from the schema of native-language learners. Despite this difference in schemas, cueing and questioning can still help students connect prior knowledge to new knowledge. Doing so might require the teacher to do something specific—which is what we explain in this chapter.

As Ovando, Collier, and Combs (2003) note, prior knowledge provides "rich clues to meaning" for students (p. 92), and cueing and questioning can be a powerful strategy for helping language learners connect knowledge presented in their new language with what they already know. Higher-level questions produce deeper learning than lower-level questions; remember that a lack of language ability is not equivalent to a lack of academic ability.

Cues and Questions: Classroom Practice Recommendations

The second edition of *Classroom Instruction That Works* offers the following recommendations for teachers as they use cueing and questioning in their classroom practice:

- Focus on what is important.
- Use explicit cues.
- Ask inferential questions.
- Ask analytic questions.

Focus on what is important. Teachers often structure cues or questions around something that they perceive as interesting or unique, under the mistaken impression that it will motivate students by piquing their interest. However, students learning English (and all other students) need to focus on what is important rather than what is unusual, and they need to be able to filter out unnecessary information to grasp the critical content. For example, to introduce a unit on the solar system, a well-intentioned 3rd grade teacher might ask students what they know about UFOs. Although the students might find the topic interesting, it does not activate students' prior knowledge about the solar system. Having any students—particularly second-language learners and other students in need of language development—focus on superfluous material will take them off track, away from the primary learning objective.

Use explicit cues. Explicit cues can help students access prior knowledge. Figure 6.1 depicts a K-W-L chart, which directly asks students what they already know about a topic. To use the K-W-L chart to provide explicit cues, the teacher might first tell students the focus of the lesson and then fill out the first column of the chart to help them recall what they already know about the topic.

K-W-L charts seem to be "just good teaching" (Harper & de Jong, 2004)—beneficial for both English language learners and non–English language learners. Nevertheless, as Harper and de Jong point out, the K-W-L chart assumes all students have the language needed to participate: the language for stating facts about what is known, the language for making a supposition about what is proposed for learning, and the language for summarizing what was learned. When teachers pay attention to language in addition to content,

FIGURE 6.1
K-W-L Chart and an Adaptation for English Language Learners

Topic: Bears

K (What I know)	W (What I want to learn)	L (What I learned)
They're brown. They're big. They live in the woods. Some are called grizzly bears.	What are baby bears called?	They hibernate in the winter. Babies are called cubs. The koala is not a bear.

K (What I know)	W (What I want to learn)	L (What I learned)
Sentence starter: I know that . . .	Sentence starter: I want to learn . . .	Sentence starter: I learned that . . .
bears growl. bears are big. bears are brown.	where they live.	bears hibernate in a cave. babies are called cubs. the koala is not a bear.

they consider the language needed to participate in a task such as the K-W-L chart and make adaptations for second-language learners, as shown in Figure 6.1. If the topic is bears, then the teacher may provide pictures for Preproduction students to point to, indicating what they already know about the topic. Early Production and Speech Emergence students could benefit from being given these sentence starters: "I know that . . . ," "I want to learn . . . ," and "I learned that . . . ." After the learning has occurred, Preproduction students could add more pictures to the final column to represent what they have learned.

Ask inferential questions. Inferential questions require students to draw conclusions, make generalizations, or call on their understanding of figurative language. Intermediate and Advanced Fluency students can make inferences in English, but Preproduction, Early Production, and Speech Emergence students, along with other students in need of language development, will have more difficulty because their levels of language acquisition limit their verbal and written output. To engage Preproduction students, ask questions that require a pointing/gesturing response. For Early Production students, ask yes/ no questions, either/or questions, or questions that require a one- or two-word response. Speech Emergence students can answer questions with a phrase or short sentence.

Ask analytic questions. Analytic questions require students to analyze errors, construct support, and analyze perspectives. Analytic questions will be challenging for students at early stages of language acquisition—again, not because of a lack of cognitive ability but because of limits on their output attributable to their stage of language acquisition. (See Chapter 2 for information on the stages of language acquisition and the Thinking Language Matrix later in this chapter for guidance on asking analytic questions.)

Adapting cues and questions for English language learners will be a new technique for many classroom teachers. As you use the cueing and questioning strategy with your students in the process of acquiring English, it's important to remember that low levels of language acquisition are not equivalent to low levels of cognitive ability. As you incorporate oral academic language instruction into the cueing and questioning strategy, remember to use cognitively appropriate cues and to ask high-level questions matched to the stage of students' second-language acquisition. In other words, plan to ask questions at all levels of Bloom's taxonomy to students in all stages of acquiring English as another language.

Thinking of high-level questions based on students' levels of second-language acquisition can be difficult to do on the spot, so you may want to consider composing questions in advance. It's unlikely that you'll have time to prepare high-level questions for students in need of language development for every lesson, every day. A more realistic goal is to identify one lesson each day to approach with prepared questions. Use the Thinking Language Matrix as a tool to identify appropriate questions for students' levels of thinking and language development.

Using the Thinking Language Matrix

As teachers build questions into their lesson planning, using the Thinking Language Matrix will provide a guide not only to students' levels of thinking on Bloom's taxonomy but also to the language supports that English language learners will need so they can answer higher-level questions. For example, we know that Early Production students can be expected to produce one-word responses and that to answer a question at the Synthesis level, students must generalize from facts. By marrying these two concepts—stage of second-language acquisition and the Bloom's taxonomy level—we can develop a question that requires students to generalize from the facts they know about a topic and produce a one-word response that indicates they have done so.

Example

An Activity Related to the Next Generation Science Standards
Grade Level: 2
Strategy: Support students in reaching proficiency in standards.

The Next Generation Science Standards expect students to construct explanations for science. To help students master this standard, a 2nd grade teacher develops an activity for a unit with the learning objective of understanding that different animals live in different environments.

For this activity, the teacher sorts her students into mixed groups of four, representing various levels of language learners, and provides each group with picture/word cards of animals:

raccoons	moles	bears
scorpions	frogs	ants
squirrels	fish	snakes
deer	ducks	lizards
worms	clams	turtles

She also provides students with a chart for sorting with pictures and names of the environments:

in lakes or oceans	in forests
in the soil	in the desert

As students are categorizing, the teacher is thinking about what higher-level analytic questions she will ask students who are at various levels of second-language acquisition. To challenge—but not frustrate—students, she knows she must ask questions at students' respective levels of second-language acquisition and, every so often, one level higher. (See the modified Thinking Language Matrix in Figure 6.2 for examples of questions at each level.)

When using the Thinking Language Matrix for cueing and questioning, involve students in generating and asking questions as a comprehension strategy. Good readers ask questions when they read, either aloud or using an inner voice. When you or your students ask lower-level questions, students will understand what a text *says*, but higher-level questions will result in students comprehending what a text *means*. Ensure that students have the opportunity to learn both what a text says and what it means by using the Question-Answer

FIGURE 6.2
Modified Thinking Language Matrix for Matching Animals to Their Environments

Levels of Thinking and Language Functions Level of thinking and academic language move from concrete recall to more complex, abstract levels.	Language Use Across Stages of Second-Language Acquisition Moves from simple to complex in grammatical tenses, forms, vocabulary, etc.				
	Preproduction: nonverbal response	**Early Production:** one-word response	**Speech Emergence:** phrases or short sentences	**Intermediate Fluency:** longer and more complex sentences	**Advanced Fluency:** near native
Evaluation appraise, argue, assess, attach, choose, compare, defend, estimate, evaluate, judge, predict, rate, select, support, value	Teacher mismatches animal with its environment and asks, "Is this the right environment? Find the right environment."	What are the best materials for the duck to build a nest?	What makes a good home for a bear? (Examine settings and evaluate, such as why a cave makes a good home.)	What would happen if you put a worm in the desert?	Recommend a different environment for a mother duck to raise her ducklings. Defend your choice.
Synthesis arrange, assemble, collect, compose, construct, create, design, develop, formulate, manage, organize, plan, prepare, propose, set up	Point to the animals that live in the soil.	Say the names of the animals that live in the soil.	How would changing the abdomen of a scorpion affect its habitat?	What would a clam need to survive in the desert?	How would you protect the wildlife in a forest where hiking was very popular?
Analysis analyze, appraise, calculate, categorize, compare, contrast, criticize, differentiate, discriminate, distinguish, examine, experiment, question, test	Show me an animal that cannot live in the forest.	Name the parts of a fish that help it live in the water.	How are raccoons and squirrels similar? How are they different?	How does a bear use its claws to catch fish? To gather berries?	Why do you think a bear hibernates in winter?

continued

FIGURE 6.2
Modified Thinking Language Matrix for Matching Animals to Their Environments
(*continued*)

	Preproduction: nonverbal response	Early Production: one-word response	Speech Emergence: phrases or short sentences	Intermediate Fluency: longer and more complex sentences	Advanced Fluency: near native
Application apply, choose, demonstrate, dramatize, employ, illustrate, interpret, operate, practice, schedule, sketch, solve, use	Show me what would happen if we put a fish in the desert.	Tell me what would happen if we put a fish in the desert.	How could you change the body of a fish to make it fly?	How would you capture and transport scorpions to a zoo?	How would a deer camouflage itself in the forest in winter? In the desert?
Comprehension classify, describe, discuss, explain, express, identify, indicate, locate, recognize, report, restate, review, select, translate	Show me where a deer lives.	Tell me which animals eat meat.	Why is a toad the color it is?	Explain how a snake catches its prey.	Why do fish need gills to live in the water? How do gills work?
Knowledge arrange, define, duplicate, label, list, name, order, recall, recognize, relate, repeat, reproduce, state	Where is the raccoon?	What is the name of this animal?	What are the body parts of a turtle?	Give the definition of a mammal.	Tell me everything you know about a clam.

Relationships (QAR) strategy, which gives teachers and students a common vocabulary for discussing four different types of questions and determining where to find answers to the questions (Urquhart & Frazee, 2012). Two of the four types of questions are text based:

- "Right There" questions are answered by searching the text and pointing to the answer. These questions begin with words or phrases such as *who, where, when, how many,* and *what kind of.*
- "Think and Search" questions are also answered by looking in the text, but students have to search for the answers, which are found in a few

different places. These questions begin with words or phrases such as *retell*, *compare*, *find examples of*, and *what caused*.

The other QARs are knowledge based, requiring students to use background knowledge:

- "Author and You" questions are answered with information that's not found in the text, but students have to have read the text to understand the question. This is an Analysis-level question on Bloom's taxonomy, so question starters could consist of *Why do you think . . . ? What motivation is there . . . ?* and *What conclusions can you draw . . . ?*
- "On My Own" questions can only be answered by using prior knowledge and do not require reading the text. Possible question starters include *Do you believe . . . ? Have you ever . . . ?* and *What would you do if . . . ?*

Opportunities to develop oral academic language

The QAR strategy gives students opportunities to interact with what they have read, which improves comprehension. When students interact with what they read, they connect what they know about the world with what they're reading in order to make sense of the text. Developing the questions requires students to speak at an academic level, and answering the questions can involve all levels of Bloom's taxonomy. Figure 6.3 shows the relationship between QAR questions and the taxonomy.

Because practicing oral academic language can increase the volume levels in the classroom, teachers need structures in place that allow them to maintain control of the classroom while allowing students to practice. The QAR strategy provides an organized approach for small groups of students to work together to develop questions for and answer questions from other student groups.

Involving students in the QAR strategy requires some upfront teaching, modeling, and think-alouds, but this initial investment of time is worth it. For students to be successful in using this strategy, teachers need to show them (model), help them (guide), let them practice together (provide practice), and let them practice independently—an approach known as the gradual release of responsibility (Duke & Pearson, 2002).

FIGURE 6.3 Bloom's Taxonomy and the QAR Strategy	
Bloom's Taxonomy	**Types of QAR Questions**
Evaluation	On My Own
Synthesis	On My Own
Application	Think and Search
Analysis	Author and You
Comprehension	Think and Search
Knowledge	Right There

To begin, introduce QAR and explain the four types of questions and answers using something familiar, such as a TV show. Think aloud with your students to formulate each type of question in a way that's focused on finding answers. Next, students can be guided in small groups to sort an array of the four types of questions into specific kinds. Student talk should focus on what type of question each is and how they decided to classify it in a certain way. During this guidance stage, you can move from the familiar to the academic while students sort questions based on text and begin to develop their own questions using question stems.

Finally, keep providing informal cooperative learning structures (see Chapter 5) so students can practice devising and responding to all four types of questions. As students become familiar with the QARs, they can also develop metaphors (see Chapter 10) for each type and represent them nonlinguistically (see Chapter 7).

Advance Organizers: Classroom Practice Recommendations

Advance organizers are organizational frameworks presented in advance of lessons that emphasize the essential ideas in a lesson or unit. They focus students on the topic at hand and help them draw connections between what they already know and the new knowledge to be learned.

Schoen and Schoen (2003) recommend the use of advance organizers for students acquiring English, noting that they help students in need of language development understand key concepts that they will be exposed to in texts. For example, when using webs, which are a kind of graphic advance organizer, students can see connections between words and phrases and the topic they are studying by following symbols and arrows.

As with cues and questions, we use advance organizers to activate and access background knowledge, prepare students for what they about to learn, and help them focus on new information. The second edition of *Classroom Instruction That Works* recommends the use of four formats for advance organizers:

- Use expository advance organizers.
- Use narrative advance organizers.
- Use skimming as an advance organizer.
- Use graphic advance organizers.

Use expository advance organizers. Expository advance organizers describe new content to be introduced in a clear-cut, uncomplicated way in verbal or written form. Although teachers of fluent English speakers might simply talk to their students about an activity and what they're going to learn, teachers of students in need of language development can't just tell their students about the lesson—they also need to show them, using sheltering techniques such as manipulatives, visuals, pantomime, facial expressions and gestures, and eye contact. Teachers also need to keep their language simple, using short sentences that rely on high-frequency vocabulary and avoiding idiomatic expressions. An expository advance organizer should be used when the content of a text is not well organized or when you want to help students focus on what they are about to learn. For students acquiring a second language, an expository advance organizer is used with informational text and includes text and pictures.

Use narrative advance organizers. Narrative advance organizers provide students with information that activates prior knowledge in an engaging way—through storytelling. Narrative advance organizers can take the form of a personal story told by the teacher, a story read aloud from a text, or even a video clip or audio story.

> **TRY THIS:** Use an expository advance organizer before a field trip.
>
> The following comments from a teacher in an East Coast school district underscore the usefulness of expository advance organizers:
>
> "I wish I would have known about this strategy before our 3rd grade field trip. It was chaos. The students thought it was a play day. They had no idea they were supposed to be learning something on the field trip."

You can use the following strategies to modify your stories to make them comprehensible to English language learners:

- Manipulatives and miniature objects
- Visuals such as photos, pictures, and drawings
- Body movement and pantomime
- Facial expressions and gestures
- Clear expression and articulation
- Short, simple sentences
- Eye contact with students
- Use of high-frequency vocabulary
- Reduction of idiomatic expressions
- Use of personalized language that favors nouns over pronouns
- Use of synonyms

Because Mr. Anderson has students at various levels of second-language acquisition in his class as well as native English speakers, he includes pictures of Gustav, Nils, and Brynhild. Mr. Anderson also displays a map so that students can trace Gustav and Nils's journey from Sweden to Minneapolis. Finally, he shows students a crown of candles and brings in St. Lucia's Day buns.

Use skimming as an advance organizer. According to Block, Gambrell, and Pressley (2002), skimming functions as "tilling the text." When students skim, they look at pictures, graphs, charts, headings and subheadings, and italicized words and phrases, which—when combined—provide them with

Example

Using a Narrative Advance Organizer
Grade Level: 3
Strategy: Use storytelling to engage students at the start of a unit.

In a unit about the experience of immigrant groups in the United States, one of the objectives is to identify obstacles and opportunities immigrants faced in the late 1800s. Before beginning the unit, Mr. Anderson tells the story of his grandfather, who emigrated from Sweden:

"My grandfather Gustav came here from Sweden with his cousin, Nils, in the late 1800s. They were young kids, 18 or 19 years old. They had been farmers in Sweden, but there was a potato famine, and thousands of Swedes immigrated to the United States about that time. I've often thought about what a spirit of adventure they must have had.

"Somehow, Grandpa Gus and cousin Nils made it to Minneapolis, where Grandpa Gus met a girl named Brynhild, whom he married. Grandma Bryn was also from Sweden. When I was little, we would go to their house to celebrate St. Lucia Day, near Christmas. One of my cousins would get to wear a beautiful white dress and a garland of lighted candles on her head. There was always a huge table full of food. One fish was very stinky, but there were also lots of delicious cookies and cakes. Like other immigrant families, we were celebrating our heritage while also making new traditions in the United States.

"Gus and Nils encountered many obstacles trying to make it in the United States, but they also had many opportunities that they didn't have back home in Sweden. We'll talk about some of the obstacles and opportunities that immigrants faced throughout this unit."

a sense of what the text is about. English language learners whose native language is similar in structure to English should skim for cognates—words that look and sound similar to English in their native language and have a similar meaning. Recognition of cognates will contribute to understanding the gist of the text and help students make connections to what they already know. For example, a 9th grade science teacher might ask his students whose first language is Spanish to scan the text for cognates—words similar in Spanish and English. Here are some examples of what the students might find: *energía gravitacional* (gravitational energy), *energía externa* (external energy), *energía enterna* (internal energy), and *isótopo radioactivo* (radioactive isotope). As they skim the English text, certain words will likely emerge because of their relationship to words in Spanish. Students may not know the meanings in English, but they may be familiar with the meanings or partial meanings in Spanish, such as *energía* (energy). Through this activity, students become aware of which physical science concepts they will be studying in the upcoming unit.

Use graphic advance organizers. A picture really *can* be worth a thousand words, particularly for students in need of language development. An effective graphic advance organizer will visually communicate what a student should learn. Teachers provide a graphic advance organizer before a lesson to prepare students for what they are about to learn and to help students direct their attention to new information. This visual map is an easy way to help students prepare for what they're expected to learn. You can provide students with graphic advance organizers that are completely or partially completed, depending on the complexity of the material and students' levels of language development.

Example

Using a Graphic Organizer to Introduce New Content
Grade Level: High school
Strategy: Provide students with a structure to organize information.

Ms. Hougham wants to introduce her high school art students to the French Impressionist painters. Before reading a chapter in their art history book that contains a number of artists' works, she presents her students with a graphic advance organizer (see Figure 6.4) that identifies some of the Impressionist painters and their works. She cues her students by encouraging them to read for additional information to add to the graphic advance organizer (such as key features of Impressionism, additional painters and paintings, and important details about either).

FIGURE 6.4
Graphic Organizer Adapted for English Language Learners

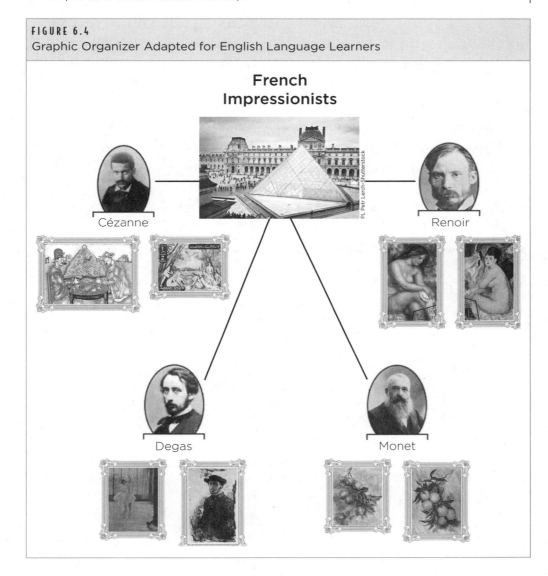

Using the Thinking Language Matrix

Use the Thinking Language Matrix to include students at all stages of second-language learning as they prepare for an upcoming field trip. The following example explains how a teacher might create the completed matrix shown in Figure 6.5.

Mrs. Hougham is now preparing her students to attend a French Impressionist exhibit at the art museum. She uses an advance graphic organizer (see Figure 6.4) to help students not only recognize the names of the paintings but also discuss the characteristics of Impressionist paintings they hope to see at the museum. Intermediate and Advanced Fluency students will share what they hope to see at the museum. Speech Emergence and Early Production students will benefit from sentence starters and the key vocabulary representing characteristics. To participate at a Comprehension level of Bloom's taxonomy, Preproduction students should be expected to listen to the discussion and classify paintings according to their characteristics.

FIGURE 6.5
Thinking Language Matrix for Advance Organizer in High School Art

Levels of Thinking and Language Functions	Tiered Thinking Across Stages of Second-Language Acquisition				
Level of thinking and academic language required for any task; move from concrete recall to more complex, abstract levels.	Language moves from simple to complex in grammatical tenses, forms, vocabulary, etc.				
	WORD $\longrightarrow$ MODEL $\longrightarrow$ EXPAND $\longrightarrow$ SOUND LIKE A BOOK				
	Preproduction: nonverbal response	**Early Production:** one-word response	**Speech Emergence:** phrases or short sentences	**Intermediate Fluency:** longer and more complex sentences	**Advanced Fluency:** near native
Comprehension classify, describe, discuss, explain, express, identify, indicate, locate, recognize, report, restate, review, select, translate	Classify paintings based on their characteristics.	Sentence starter: I hope to see _____. Vocabulary: brushstrokes, lines, color, lighting		"I hope to see examples of everyday life." "I want to take a good look at the brushstrokes."	

Opportunities to develop oral academic language

No advance organizer is going to prepare culturally and linguistically diverse students and other students in need of language development for upcoming information, help them focus on new content, or help them develop oral academic language if they do not understand the vocabulary that accompanies the advance organizer. Therefore, you need to preteach vocabulary before students encounter it in text or in advance organizers.

How will you decide which words to preteach? One possible approach is to consider the three tiers of vocabulary development identified by Beck, McKeown, and Kucan (2002). Tier 1 words are basic words occurring in everyday speech; Tier 2 words are those that frequently occur across content areas; and Tier 3 words are less frequent and appear in few content areas. Although Beck and her colleagues did not develop these three tiers specifically for teaching vocabulary to students acquiring English as another language, the tiers provide a good starting point for thinking about which words might need to be pretaught to emerging English users.

Once you've determined in which tier a word falls, you can then use a five-step approach to preteach it (Marzano et al., 2001). Remember that as you advance in the tier levels, students may need more time and support to develop an understanding of the word's meaning. Here are the five steps:

1. Provide students with a brief description or explanation (not a dictionary definition) of the new vocabulary word or term in student-friendly language.
2. Give students a nonlinguistic representation to accompany the word in the form of a picture, graphic organizer, mental image, physical representation, or kinesthetic representation (see Chapter 7).
3. Ask students to create a description or explanation of the word in their own words. To foster opportunities for oral academic language development, have students share their explanations with partners or in a small group.
4. Ask students to construct a nonlinguistic representation to accompany the word.

5. Provide time to review the accuracy of descriptions and representations. For students in need of language development, create opportunities for this review to occur in the context of productive academic talk.

After preteaching the vocabulary associated with each of the four types of advance organizers, you're ready to use them with your students.

Example

Preteaching Vocabulary Before Using an Advance Organizer
Grade Level: 2
Strategy: Help students organize their thinking.

Ms. Mackenzie's 2nd grade class is going on a field trip to a butterfly pavilion. She prepares them for the onslaught of stimuli they are about to receive by showing and explaining the focus: the life cycle of a butterfly.

Before the field trip, Ms. Mackenzie may need to preteach Tier 1, 2, and 3 words. To be thoughtful and systematic in the selection of words to preteach, she can ask herself these questions (Herrara, Perez, & Escamilla, 2010):

- What are the Tier 3 words that are essential to students in the process of learning English for understanding the key concepts that are the focus of the lesson? (*larva, pupa*)

- Are any of these words cognates? (Are they found in languages with a Greek–Latin base such as Spanish, Portugese, Italian, French, Greek, or Romanian?) (*larva*)

- Which Tier 2 words are important for comprehending the topic and could be confusing because they occur in other content areas? (*cycle*)

- Which Tier 1 words are relevant and can be taught using nonlinguistic representations? (*butterfly, wings, change*).

- What background knowledge might my students learning English have related to this topic?

After preteaching the vocabulary essential to the expository advance organizer, Ms. Mackenzie can use the organizer to activate and access students' background knowledge and provide them with a way to organize their thinking around the content they are about to encounter.

Tips for Teaching Using Cues, Questions, and Advance Organizers

- Asking higher-level questions of second-language learners and others in need of language development requires advance planning. Collaborate with other teachers in your building to create a central electronic repository where all teachers can share higher-level questions, related to topics in the curriculum, that link the stages of second-language acquisition with Bloom's taxonomy.

- Ask a colleague to script the questions you ask during a lesson. Place the questions into the Thinking Language Matrix and make observations about your use of questions. For example, look at the level of questions you asked students acquiring English as another language. Did you ask high-level questions of all English language learners, regardless of their stage of language acquisition? If not, work at developing higher-level questions based on students' stages of second-language acquisition. After a period of time, ask a colleague to script you again and place the questions into the matrix. Reflect on the extent to which you improved your practice.

- If you think a textbook is not well organized, use one of the four advance organizers before asking students to read it. The advance organizer should be designed to give the text organization and clarity.

7

Nonlinguistic Representations

Imagine that you're visiting another country and a local asks you what you do for a living. Will you know enough of the language to describe your occupation? Perhaps not, but chances are that you'd be able to draw a picture to represent it. That's the power of nonlinguistic representations.

Knowledge is stored in two ways: linguistically and nonlinguistically. Teachers typically present new knowledge linguistically, asking students to read or listen to new information. Think of knowledge presented linguistically as actual sentences stored in long-term memory. Nonlinguistic representations, by contrast, are stored as mental pictures. Because many English-language-learning students know what they want to say to represent their thinking in their native language but do not have enough English to do so, nonlinguistic methods of learning and communicating are particularly important for them. Nonlinguistic representations not only help teachers provide information to students acquiring English but also help them get a fuller idea of the knowledge that students possess when they do not have all of the words to describe it.

Dual-coding theory supports the use of nonlinguistic representations in conjunction with linguistic representations as a means of recalling knowledge (Paivio, 2006). That is, when students listen to or read text, the left side of the brain registers high activity as it stores information verbally in words and sentences; when they are asked to use their senses and body parts to register knowledge (for example, creating a "movie in the mind"), it's the right side of the brain that registers activity as it stores information nonverbally with a nonlinguistic representation. If students store knowledge in both ways, they will be better able to recall and use the knowledge.

Nonlinguistic Representations: Classroom Practice Recommendations

The second edition of *Classroom Instruction That Works* has five recommendations for classroom practice with nonlinguistic representations. Students should have opportunities to

- Use graphic organizers.
- Make physical models or use manipulatives.
- Generate mental pictures.
- Create pictures, illustrations, and pictographs.
- Engage in kinesthetic activities.

Use graphic organizers. Graphic organizers, which include Venn diagrams, charts, webs, and timelines, can be designed to make complex content more understandable for second-language learners. (See Chapter 8 for descriptions of the primary types of graphic organizers.) For example, textbooks are often too complicated for students in the process of acquiring English. Graphic organizers can present the information from a text in a way that helps students better understand and store the information. Keep in mind that you may need to teach your students how to use graphic organizers. When introducing graphic organizers, use familiar content so students can focus on the process of using the organizer without simultaneously having to learn new content (Karpicke & Roediger, 2008).

Example

Completing an Episode Graphic Organizer
Grade Level: 5
Strategy: Teach students how to use a graphic organizer.

Mr. Reid's 5th grade class is studying the Boston Tea Party. In addition to the text the class is reading together, they also complete an episode graphic organizer that includes the key events, people, and timeline associated with the event. Mr. Reid models the use of the episode graphic organizer by verbalizing his thoughts as he works with the class to fill in its various parts. Students elaborate on their knowledge by working individually to add pictures to the organizer. Eventually, students will be expected to use episode graphic organizers independently to depict historical events.

Make physical models or use manipulatives. Physical models are concrete representations of what students are learning. Although the use of manipulatives is commonly associated with mathematics (when learning about shapes or money, for example), manipulatives can be incorporated in all content areas through items such as puzzles, maps, word sorts, and building blocks. For example, during a geography lesson, instead of labeling the 50 states on a worksheet, students might assemble a puzzle made up of pieces that represent each state. Any three-dimensional form can be a physical model. For culturally and linguistically diverse students and others in need of language development, the very act of constructing a concrete representation establishes an image of the knowledge, and they don't have to depend solely on words. For example, a student acquiring English as another language may not have the words to describe how an electric current works but can relate knowledge by acting out the process.

Example

> **Using Manipulatives**
> **Grade Level:** 6
> **Strategy:** Help students recall and use information.

A 6th grade music curriculum includes the science of sound and musical instruments. For English language learners to be able to recall and use information about the structure of the ear, the teacher provides materials so students can construct and label the outer, middle, and inner ear. Students are introduced to each part of the ear as they build it and discover how all of the parts work together in order to hear sounds. Students then use the parts of the ear again when they learn about how sounds travel.

Generate mental pictures. When emerging English users listen or read, creating a "movie in the mind" helps them understand and store knowledge. Using all five senses can help produce mental images. Again, start with familiar content when teaching a new process. For example, ask students to picture lunchtime in the cafeteria. What do they see? Can they see students sitting at tables, eating their lunches, laughing, and talking? Can they see cafeteria workers busy in the kitchen, dishing out food and cleaning trays? You can take this activity one step further by actually sitting with your students in the cafeteria and asking them what they see. Next, have them close their eyes and envision the same things. With their eyes closed, what do they hear? What do they smell? Ask them to take a bite of different lunch items and describe each one with their eyes closed. How did it taste? Finally, ask students how they feel in the lunchroom, starting with climate (Is it hot? Cold? Humid?) and moving to emotions (Are they happy to be out of class? Intimidated by the noise and number of people?). Other familiar contexts you can use when helping students use their five senses include getting to school, recess, the opening of the school day (for elementary students), and pep rallies (for secondary students).

After practicing in familiar contexts, you can try this exercise in academic contexts. For example, a 5th grade history and social studies teacher might ask students learning about Marco Polo and the Silk Route to imagine being in the explorer's place. The teacher sets the scene: "It's July, it's hot, it's dusty, and the road—no more than a footpath—goes on forever. What do you hear as you walk? The wind? Animals? What do you smell? Sweat? Animals again? What do you feel? Are you sweaty, thirsty, hungry, or tired? Do your feet hurt? Do you have sunburn? What can you taste? Is your mouth dry?" The teacher then gives students time to craft a movie in their minds and share it with their partners. After numerous guided practices, the teacher begins to decrease the amount of guidance so that students can generate their own visualizations.

Students acquiring English and others in need of language development may need reminders on how to involve all of their senses when creating a movie in the mind. Figure 7.1 provides one way to remind them.

FIGURE 7.1
Involving All Senses to Create a Movie in the Mind

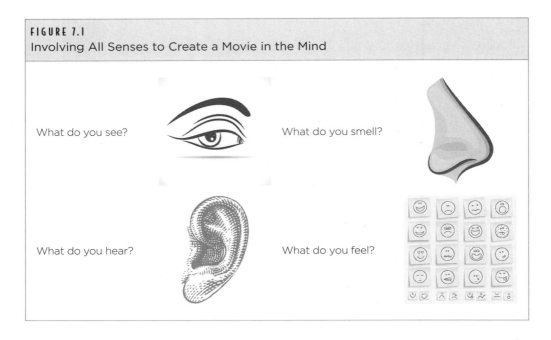

What do you see?

What do you smell?

What do you hear?

What do you feel?

As a comprehension strategy, asking students to make a movie in their minds is a purposeful way they can interact with text to construct meaning. Generating mental pictures is the same as visualizing—a reading strategy that makes reading and talking about what has been read more fun and motivating.

Create pictures, illustrations, and pictographs. All students benefit from opportunities to represent knowledge using pictures, illustrations, and pictographs. For second-language-acquisition students, such opportunities are critical because they provide a way for them to represent and elaborate on what they know. This is especially important for students in the early stages of second-language acquisition (see Preproduction and Early Production stages in Chapter 2). In addition, many culturally and linguistically diverse students enter the U.S. school system with background knowledge in their primary languages. Showing students pictures and pictographs related to this knowledge can help them bridge the language gap.

Example

> **Representing Vocabulary Terms with Nonlinguistic Representations**
> **Grade Level:** 7
> **Strategy:** Teach vocabulary via words and pictures.

A middle school teacher is teaching a 7th grade exploratory class on financial literacy with many English language learners. Rather than teaching the terms *value*, *want*, *need*, and *goal* to only the linguistic side of the brain by using definitions, the teacher asks students to find or draw pictures that represent the four vocabulary terms. The pictures can be reused for classification (sorting) activities.

Engage in kinesthetic activities. Total Physical Response (TPR) has long been a popular approach to teaching students acquiring English as another language. Developed by James Asher (1969), TPR uses kinesthetic activities to teach English. Students engage in active language learning by demonstrating their comprehension through body movements. In early lessons, students are directed to stand up, turn around, sit down, or clap their hands. More complex commands follow, with participants eventually verbalizing commands to the instructor and their classmates.

A 4th grade math teacher wants students to learn a math term by saying the word as they use their arms to represent the term. The teacher models by saying "radius of a circle" and extending one arm from her side to represent a line from the center of the circle to the outside of the circle. Students imitate. Throughout the unit of study, whenever students encounter the term, they attach the arm movement. Eventually, the teacher notices that her students are using their arms as they take a mathematics test, and she knows they have internalized the knowledge. Other math terms suitable for modeling and imitation include the *diameter* of a circle, the *circumference* of a circle, an *acute* angle, an *obtuse* angle, and a *right* angle. Students are better able to recall and use what they have learned by combining the kinesthetic activity (nonlinguistic representation) with the mathematics term (linguistic representation).

If emerging English users are to use the five different types of nonlinguistic representations to store and retrieve information, elaborate on knowledge, and "show what they know," then they need multiple examples modeled by the teacher with accompanying think-alouds (verbalizations of the teacher's thinking as the representation is completed). Remember that words alone don't convey meaning.

When teachers rely on lecture and text to communicate knowledge, skills, and processes, students who are learning English won't receive the intended message in its entirety. All of the words coming from a teacher's mouth and all of the words written in a text won't be fully understood until a student learning English reaches the Advanced Fluency level of second-language acquisition (as described in Chapter 2). Second-language learners will be working hard to make sense of and store the verbal information they receive using the left side of their brains. If teachers add one or more of the five types of nonlinguistic representations to what they are saying or what students are reading, English language learners and others in need of language development will be better able to store and retrieve the expected knowledge or skills and processes.

Students in the process of acquiring English may not understand the teacher's message when only words are used because the student is still in the process of learning English. Rather, culturally and linguistically diverse students have a better chance of comprehending teacher talk or what they've read when they can also see it represented with graphic organizers or as three-dimensional models, movies in the mind, pictures in a sequence of movements, or a dramatic presentation.

Using the Thinking Language Matrix

The Thinking Language Matrix can be used to help English-language-learning students at all stages of acquisition use nonlinguistic representations to explain their thinking. Not only is it important for them to use nonlinguistic representations to accompany their work, it is equally important for them

> **TRY THIS:** Use any of the five types of nonlinguistic representations.
>
> ---
>
> Teachers report that when students return as adults to visit, these former students recall the times they built something in class or acted out something in class more than the essays they wrote. In other words, they remember when they were required to use both sides of their brain rather than only the linguistic side.

to verbally explain their nonlinguistic representation as another form of elaboration and as a means of fostering oral language. In the activity described in the following paragraph, students are asked to represent what they know by creating a drawing and comparing it to another one. This activity is at the Evaluation level on Bloom's taxonomy, as students present opinions based on a set of criteria established by making comparisons. The example explains how a teacher might use the process to create the completed matrix shown in Figure 7.2.

Students in a 7th grade language arts class are about to read a novel in which much of the action takes place in a bookstore. To build background knowledge for students, the teacher takes them on a field trip to a bookstore (or has them view a video of a local bookstore). Students are then asked to draw the inside of the bookstore, including the location and types of books, computers, children's section, and other elements. Students explain their non-linguistic representations to other students. Next, students read the description of the bookstore in the novel and draw a picture using the description provided. Students then compare the bookstore they visited to the one in the novel and explain their comparisons to other students.

Using nonlinguistic representations to compare and explain helps students elaborate on knowledge and brings them to a higher level of thinking. For example, Preproduction students are expected to work at the Evaluation level of Bloom's taxonomy as they form opinions about similarities and differences in the two drawings (such as the number of steps a customer has to climb to make a purchase or the ideal size and shape of the bookstore). Because their thinking is at an evaluative level and their verbal output is at a nonverbal stage,

FIGURE 7.2
Thinking Language Matrix for 7th Grade Language Arts Bookstore Activity

Levels of Thinking and Language Functions	Tiered Thinking Across Stages of Second-Language Acquisition				
Level of thinking and academic language required for any task; move from concrete recall to more complex, abstract levels.	Language moves from simple to complex in grammatical tenses, forms, vocabulary, etc.				
	WORD ⟶ MODEL ⟶ EXPAND ⟶ SOUND LIKE A BOOK				
	Preproduction: nonverbal response	Early Production: one-word response	Speech Emergence: phrases or short sentences	Intermediate Fluency: longer and more complex sentences	Advanced Fluency: near native
Evaluation appraise, argue, assess, attach, choose, compare, defend, estimate, evaluate, judge, predict, rate, select, support, value	Students draw a picture of a real bookstore. Using a picture another student has drawn of a fictional bookstore, they then compare the two, using the following steps: 1. Select the items to compare. 2. Identify the characteristics of the items on which to base your comparison. 3. Explain how the items are similar to and different from each other, with respect to the characteristics you identified. Students can then use plus and minus symbols to show similarities and differences.	Students draw in detail a real and fictional bookstore and compare the two drawings. Students use the following steps for comparing to explain their two pictures: 1. Select the items to compare. 2. Identify the characteristics of the items on which to base your comparison. 3. Explain how the items are similar to and different from each other, with respect to the characteristics you identified. Sentence starter: When I compare the _____ in the stores, they are alike because _____.		Students draw in detail a real and fictional bookstore and compare the two drawings. Students use the following steps for comparing to explain their two pictures: 1. Select the items to compare. 2. Identify the characteristics of the items on which to base your comparison. 3. Explain how the items are similar to and different from each other, with respect to the characteristics you identified.	

they can use plus and minus symbols to express their views. Early Production and Speech Emergence students, having more language available, will convey their judgments with sentence starters. Intermediate and Advanced Fluency students possess the most language, so they should be expected to use longer and more complex sentences with higher-level vocabulary rather than short disconnected phrases with everyday language.

Opportunities to develop oral academic language

Let's look at how teachers can foster English language proficiency as part of subject-matter instruction using this strategy.

Once students begin using the five types of nonlinguistic representations to represent and elaborate on knowledge, they should be expected to talk about them, answering questions such as these: *Why did you select that particular graphic organizer to accompany what you are reading? What does that picture mean?* Students can talk with others about their representations.

For teachers of content, language may seem invisible: you *teach with* language but you do not actually *teach* language. Many teachers, particularly secondary teachers, focus on mastery of content and are not aware of the language learning that needs to occur in conjunction with the subject matter. To help make the shift from teaching content alone to supporting language in addition to the academic subject areas, it's useful to think about language as an action. Students learn a language as they use a language. Because teachers are being asked to support rich oral academic language in addition to content, they should purposefully plan for student-to-student interaction and note it in their lesson plans. Keep in mind that interaction is fundamental to second-language acquisition. Whenever you plan for accountable student talk time (see Chapter 5 for structures you can use), you are supporting the learning of English alongside the learning of academic subject matter. Just as the content is academic, so is the talk. Talking is not an end in itself; it must be structured to elicit rich oral academic language from second-language learners and others in need of language development. What lens can you use to filter the talk taking place? How can you consider the language you hear and verify that it is the level of academic language you are seeking? To begin with, ask yourself these questions:

- Is it conversational language? In other words, does it sound like language used after school with friends and at home?
- Is it academic language? Do students sound like a book?

To influence the use of classroom language (i.e., language used on tests), plan for how students can use a higher-level repertoire of language than the language they use on the playground. If students use a chronological graphic organizer to recap a sequence of events, plan for them to use the language of sequencing: *initially, meanwhile, preceding*. Let students know which words you expect to hear them use while they are describing the order of events displayed in their graphic organizers. Model it first. For example, a chemistry teacher wants his students to structure the steps of an experiment for their lab reports by using a chronological graphic organizer. As students work in small groups, they are expected to use the language of sequencing, as the teacher does when he tells the students what he wants them to do: "*Preceding* the experiment, put on your apron and goggles." "*Initially*, you place three beakers together." "*Meanwhile*, you are heating the water."

In the Next Generation Science Standards, students are expected to construct explanations and communicate ideas, concepts, and information related to a phenomenon or system (natural or designed). The Academic Language Framework shown in Figure 7.3 presents one way to help students develop oral academic language while addressing that standard in an 8th grade lesson on the solar system.

The 8th grade science teacher whose work is represented in the framework has "gone to the balcony" to get a big-picture view of the class when the students are engaged in the task of describing the relationship between the motion of objects in the solar system and the phenomena of days, years, eclipses, phases of the moon, and seasons. The teacher is visualizing students engaged in this task and considers what rich oral academic language (exemplars) should be used when describing motion:

- "The sun is the center of the solar system."
- "The planets revolve around the sun."
- "Earth rotates on its axis."

FIGURE 7.3
Academic Language Framework for an 8th Grade Science Lesson

Task	Exemplars	Academic Language			
		Function of Language	Vocabulary	Grammar	Sentence Starter(s)
Describe the relationship between motion of objects in the solar system and the phenomena of days, years, eclipses, phases of the moon, and seasons.	Background "The sun is the center of the solar system." "The planets revolve around the sun." "Earth rotates on its axis." Day "Earth's rotation creates day and night." "It takes Earth 24 hours to make one complete rotation." Year "It takes one year for Earth to completely revolve around the sun."	describing relationships	Background *orbit, axis, eclipse, phase* Word Families *revolve, revolution; rotate, rotation*	*if . . . then* common/proper nouns possessives	*If* Earth blocks sunlight from reflecting off the moon's surface, *then* it is a _____. *If* the moon blocks sunlight from reaching Earth, then it is a _____. If the _____ blocks _____, *then* _____ happens. (optional word bank: *sun, moon, Earth, eclipse*)

From this bird's-eye view of the class, the teacher can now think about the academic language of science. The teacher is going to reflect on the function of language and why students are talking in small groups: to describe relationships. Next, she thinks about what English language learners will need to engage in the descriptions selected as exemplars, such as the following:

- **Vocabulary**—key words needed to engage in the standard: *orbit, axis, eclipse, phase*; word families: *revolve, revolution; rotate, rotation.*
- **Grammar**—grammatical structures and parts of speech: *if . . . then*, common and proper nouns, possessives.
- **Sentence starters**—If Earth blocks sunlight from reflecting off the moon's surface, then it is a _____. (*lunar eclipse*)

By identifying the function of language along with vocabulary, grammar, and sentence starters, the teacher becomes better able to support language in addition to content in this science lesson. In this lesson, culturally and linguistically diverse students can use the strategy of nonlinguistic representations—they can act out eclipses and rotations while talking about the relationships.

Tips for Teaching Using Nonlinguistic Representations

- Think about the gradual release of responsibility model (Fisher & Frey, 2008), whereby you introduce knowledge and students then apply it. Fisher and Frey refer to this structure for successful instruction as "I do it," "We do it," "You do it together," and "You do it alone." In the teacher responsibility phase, when you're helping students acquire and integrate knowledge, are you primarily lecturing? With students in the process of learning English in the classroom, words alone do not convey meaning, so add one or more of the nonlinguistic representations to what you are saying to assist with understanding.
- For one week, keep a tally of the nonlinguistic representations you're using to accompany what you're saying and what students are reading. Which of the five types of nonlinguistic representations do you use most? The least? Set a goal for yourself to incorporate additional use of the nonlinguistic representations you are not currently using frequently.
- Keep track of the nonlinguistic representations you ask students to add to their work so that they are better able to recall and use what they have learned. Which of the five are they using the most? The least? If you find that they're using only one or two, consider expanding your students' repertoire of nonlinguistic representations.

8

Summarizing and Note Taking

Think back to the last time you had to take notes or summarize information—perhaps from your last staff meeting. Did you give much thought to how you might capture the information you needed? If you went back to your notes from that event, would you be able to make sense of them today?

Often, we think of summarizing and note taking as innate skills that everyone just somehow knows. However, for mainstream students and students in need of language development alike, note taking and summarizing can be far from intuitive. The research is clear that these skills matter—the updated meta-analysis for the second edition of *Classroom Instruction That Works* found that both summarizing and note taking positively affect student achievement across grade levels and content areas, with a higher effect size for note taking than for summarizing (Beesley & Apthorp, 2010).

Summarizing: Classroom Practice Recommendations

Students know that they need to summarize to condense information, but they don't always have a good method for doing so. Here are the three recommendations from the second edition of *Classroom Instruction That Works*:

- Teach students the rule-based summarizing strategy.
- Use summary frames.
- Engage students in reciprocal teaching.

Teach students the rule-based summarizing strategy. The rule-based summarizing strategy provides a set of guidelines to help students understand what information to focus on and what information to discard when summarizing (Dean et al., 2012). The rules are as follows:

1. Take out material that is not important to understanding.
2. Take out words that repeat information.
3. Replace a list of things with one word that describes them (e.g., replace "oak, elm, and maple" with "trees").
4. Find a topic sentence, or create one if it is missing.

Again, as is always the case when presenting a new process, it helps to begin with familiar content. When teachers are presenting a difficult concept such as summarizing, adding a metaphor, simile, or analogy (see Chapter 10) will help attach the new learning to what is already known and familiar. In other words, students will better understand summarizing if they can cognitively picture how to summarize.

Can you see the following analogy? While washing the dishes, a teacher realized that the sponge held a sufficient amount of water, but when squeezed, it still held enough to wipe down the counter. It occurred to her that a sponge was like a summary in that "we take hold of saturated text and squeeze out all the unnecessary details, keeping only what we need to get the idea across" (Rader, n.d.). When introducing summarizing to her students, she dunked a sponge in water and, while squeezing out the water, said, "I'm summarizing" and passed around the damp sponge. After modeling the rule-based summarization process, she asked students to explain why a sponge is like a summary.

Example

Summarizing Using Kinesthetic Gestures
Grade Level: Middle school
Strategy: Teach students the rules for summarizing.

A middle school teacher wants students to learn the rules for summarizing and knows his words alone will not convey meaning. Therefore, he adds the nonlinguistic representation known as kinesthetic representation (see Chapter 7) to what he is saying to assist

English language learners with understanding. As he explains the rule-based strategy for summarizing, he includes these gestures with the key words:

Key Word	Gesture
keep	Pull hands in to chest.
delete	Push hands away from body.
substitute	Cross hands to show movement.

By modeling the gestures that accompany the verbal rules to keep, delete, or substitute information, the teacher is making the rules more comprehensible to a student who is learning English. A teacher can encourage all students to add the gestures if they are explaining what they did to keep, delete, or substitute information. This helps to store the rules on both sides of the brain, so they can be accessed more easily in the future when summarizing.

Use summary frames. Summary frames are a series of questions that highlight critical elements from specific text patterns. Students use the answers to the questions to formulate a summary. The second edition of *Classroom Instruction That Works* identifies six types of summary frames: (1) narrative, (2) topic-restriction-illustration, (3) definition, (4) argumentation, (5) problem-solution, and (6) conversation. However, because these summary frames rely heavily on text, they don't always readily lend themselves to instructing English language learners, particularly Preproduction and Speech Emergence students. For second-language learners and others in need of language development, summary frames require nonlinguistic representation.

To make summary frames user-friendly for students acquiring English and others in need of language development, we have adapted and applied the concept to six patterns of informational text identified in the third edition of *Teaching Reading in the Content Areas* (Urquhart & Frazee, 2012). Typically, informational (or expository) text is written to inform or persuade (examples include textbook chapters, newspaper and magazine articles, and reference materials). Each of the six common patterns of informational text has an associated graphic organizer (as shown in Appendix D) and signal, or transition, words (Jones, Palincsar, Ogle, & Carr, 1987; Marzano & Pickering, 1997).

The six text patterns and their accompanying signal words, as described in *Teaching Reading in the Content Areas* (Urquhart & Frazee, 2012, pp. 26–27), are as follows:

- **Sequence:** Organizes events in a logical sequence, usually chronological. **Signal words:** *after, afterward, as soon as, before, during, finally, first, following, immediately, initially, later, meanwhile, next, not long after, now, on (date), preceding, second, soon, then, third, today, until, when.*
- **Comparison/contrast:** Organizes information about two or more topics according to their similarities and differences. **Signal words:** *although, as well as, as opposed to, both, but, compared with, different from, either, even though, however, instead of, in common, on the other hand, otherwise, similarly, still yet.*
- **Concept/definition:** Organizes information about a word or phrase that represents a generalized idea of a class of people, places, things, and events (e.g., dictatorship, economics, culture, mass production). Concept/definition text defines a concept by presenting its characteristics or attributes. **Signal words:** *for instance, in other words, is characterized by, put another way, refers to, that is, thus, usually.*
- **Description:** Organizes facts that describe the characteristics of specific people, places, things, and events. These characteristics can appear in any order. **Signal words:** *above, across, along, appears to be, as in, behind, below, beside, between, down, in back of, in front of, looks like, near, on top of, onto, outside, over, such as, to the right/left, under.*
- **Episode:** Organizes a large body of information about specific events including time and place, people, duration, sequence, and causes and effects. **Signal words:** *a few days/months later, around this time, as it is often called, as a result of, because of, began, when, consequently, first, for this reason, lasted for, led to, shortly thereafter, since, then, subsequently, this led to, when.*
- **Generalization/principle:** Organizes information into general statements with supporting examples. **Signal words:** *additionally, always, as a*

result, because of, clearly, conclusively, first, for instance, for example, further-more, generally, however, if . . . then, in fact, it could be argued that, moreover, most convincing, never, not only . . . but also, often, second, therefore, third, truly, typically.

According to Short (1994), when second-language-acquisition students are taught to understand text patterns and recognize the signal words accompanying them, reading and writing skills improve. Signal words are examples of rich oral academic English because many of them are words that aren't typically used in conversation. When students use them orally or in written language, they are moving closer to sounding like a book.

When we provide students with summary frames and associated signal words and graphic organizers, we're offering them several tools for summarizing. Students can complete the graphic organizer according to the type of text they are reading, and they can answer the questions that accompany the way a text is organized. Both the graphic organizer and the answers to the questions will help English-learning-language students formulate their summaries. Using text patterns for summarizing is especially beneficial for students who have reached at least a Speech Emergence level of second-language acquisition. Examples of all six patterns used for summarizing appear in Appendix D.

TRY THIS: Introduce Pairs Reading and summarizing.

To construct meaning, students must interact with the text. One of the authors, having worked with the Commonwealth of the Northern Mariana Islands public school system through the Striving Readers Comprehensive Literacy Grant, reports a teacher's success with an interactive approach called Pairs Reading. Students collaborate to help one another understand the text by reading aloud. While one student reads aloud, another listens and then summarizes what he or she heard (Urquhart & Frazee, 2012). The teacher is mindful of the need to build the oral language proficiency of her English language learners as a prerequisite to developing strong writing skills for summarization. Because the majority of her students range from Speech

Emergence to Advanced Fluency, she knows that when students have the opportunity to verbalize a summary, they will be better prepared and have the words necessary for writing the summary independently when they return to their desks after the pair work.

Here's what one teacher has to say about this approach:

1st Try: The students thought I was crazy, and I was not sure how this would turn out, but it was great! I like how the students listening do not read; they just listen and then summarize. We will do this often!

2nd Try: Tried it with science this time. It was great to see the students reread without me having to ask them. I did not let the readers clarify; they could reread twice and then help if needed. At the end, students wrote a summary together of everything they read.

3rd Try: We read biographies on various historical people. Once again, it was great.

Engage students in reciprocal teaching. Reciprocal teaching is an instructional activity that helps students understand what they have read. During reciprocal teaching (which we described in Chapter 3), a small group of students carry out four specific roles after reading a portion of expository text: summarizing, questioning, clarifying, and predicting. Before students can perform the roles, the teacher models each one.

Any teacher with English language learners and others in need of language development should designate purposeful instructional time for this modeling. The teacher should demonstrate how to perform the role and think aloud as he or she applies the role to a portion of expository text. Instructing students in one strategy per day for four days is one way to roll out this approach to constructing meaning from text.

While explaining each role, the teacher should add a nonlinguistic representation and provide sentence starters that are useful when assuming the role. Pictures are an important support for English language learners; rather than just seeing the written role of summarizer, for example, they also see a pictorial representation of it. After students have had opportunities to connect the written word to the picture, the picture can be removed. The same scaffold, or system of support, should be made available in the form of sentence starters. After English language learners have had many occasions to hear others use the sentence starters and have used them numerous times themselves, the teacher can minimize use of this learning aid. The following example expands Rader's sponge analogy to include all four roles of reciprocal teaching.

Example

Reciprocal Teaching
Grade Level: Elementary
Strategy: Use nonlinguistic representations and sentence starters to explain the four roles of reciprocal teaching.

Step 1: Explain reciprocal teaching roles to students, as follows.

 A sponge is like a summary. Let's take this sponge and dunk it into this pail of water. Now I'm going to squeeze it out. You will do the same when you summarize. Take what you read and squeeze out everything except the most important person, place, thing, or event. The sponge has just enough moisture to wipe the table. Leave just enough details in your summary so we know what is good to know about your important person, place, thing, or event. When you are the summarizer, you can say things such as this:

- The most important person/place/thing/event is _____.
- The most important idea about the person/place/thing/event is _____.
- Does anyone want to add to my summary?

A picture of a question mark can represent the role of questioner and asking questions about what has been read. You should ask questions that will make others think about what they have read:

- Why _____?
- How _____?
- Explain _____.
- Would anyone else like to ask a question?

When you're the clarifier, you will think about using a magnifying glass because a magnifying glass helps us see things close up. As the clarifier, you will examine what you just read and look for something that could be confusing to others. The clarifier can find vocabulary words that might be confusing. You can ask others if there is anything they need clarified. The clarifier can say things such as this:

- Here is an idea I would like to clarify.
- _____ means _____.
- Is there anything else to clarify?

When you are the predictor, you are like someone with a crystal ball. You will predict what the author will tell us next. The predictor says things such as this:

- I think _____ will happen next.
- I predict the author will tell us _____.
- I predict the next part will be about _____.
- What do you predict?

Step 2: Students practice the roles with the teacher. Teacher and students practice the roles one at a time after reading a portion of informational text. Once students are ready to assume the roles, each student can be provided with a name tent. One side of the name tent will show the name of the student's role along with a nonlinguistic representation; the other side will contain appropriate sentence starters. Once students become proficient with the roles, they will not need this scaffold.

Step 3: After the teacher has demonstrated the four roles and the students are showing competency, the teacher divides the class into "home" groups of four, with each student assigned to be a summarizer, questioner, clarifier, or predictor. Teachers and students read a section of text as a group. All of the summarizers then meet in one corner of the room, as do the questioners, clarifiers, and predictors. The summarizers collaboratively decide on the summary they will take to their home groups. All of the questioners determine the questions to ask their home groups about what they read. The clarifiers jointly agree on what needs to be clarified. The predictors return and share their projections with their home groups after they have jointly settled on a common prediction. Everyone returns to the home groups with the same ideas.

Step 4: After students demonstrate mastery in their assigned roles, they may not need the support of their "corner" groups and can initiate the roles on their own.

Each of the four roles represents what successful readers do on their own when they read. Eventually, we want students to internalize the four roles or reading strategies and use them when reading independently.

TRY THIS: Use reciprocal teaching with writing.

Reciprocal teaching can also be used with writing. After a written language assignment, each group of four students selects one of their papers to read as a group. The author of the paper serves as summarizer and summarizes what was written for the other three.

The questioner looks for any missing information and asks applicable questions. Anyone in the group can answer the questions and ask questions themselves. The clarifier looks for anything that is not clear and may say, "I wonder what you meant by . . ." The author and any of the others in the group can respond, and anyone may ask for additional clarification. The predictor suggests what the author could write about next and can ask others in the group to contribute as well.

Using the Thinking Language Matrix

The Thinking Language Matrix can be used to include English-language-learning students at all stages of language acquisition in the summarizing process. Summarizing is a robust activity with many subskills, each of which needs to be introduced to and practiced by English language learners. Because summarizing is a form of Synthesis, students are working at a high level of thinking on Bloom's taxonomy during this process. The example that follows explains how a teacher might use the process to create the completed matrix shown in Figure 8.1.

A 4th grade teacher has broken down the rule-based summarizing strategy into the following steps:

1. Take out material that is not important to understanding.
2. Take out words that repeat information.
3. Replace a list of things with one word that describes all of them.
4. Find a topic sentence, or create one if it is missing.

This teacher has provided explicit instruction in all of the steps, and the students are now ready to use them to write a summary. The teacher provides students with a familiar and engaging nonfiction text for them to summarize. Each student writes a summary and reads it to a partner who then provides feedback on the summary based on the four steps.

FIGURE 8.1					
Thinking Language Matrix for Summarizing					

Levels of Thinking and Language Functions	**Tiered Thinking Across Stages of Second-Language Acquisition**				
Level of thinking and academic language required for any task; move from concrete recall to more complex, abstract levels.	Language moves from simple to complex in grammatical tenses, forms, vocabulary, etc.				
	WORD ⟶ MODEL ⟶ EXPAND ⟶ SOUND LIKE A BOOK				
	Preproduction: nonverbal response	**Early Production:** one-word response	**Speech Emergence:** phrases or short sentences	**Intermediate Fluency:** longer and more complex sentences	**Advanced Fluency:** near native
Synthesis arrange, assemble, collect, compose, construct, create, design, develop, formulate, manage, organize, plan, prepare, propose, set up	Students assemble words into the correct order using a topic sentence that has been cut apart.	Sentence starter: Your topic sentence _____. Student chooses from the following options: • has everything in it. • is missing some important ideas. • has too many details in it.		"You left out an important part in your topic sentence."	

Opportunities to develop oral academic language

Repeating information is critical to student understanding (Medina, 2008), and summarizing is one way for students to repeat what they've learned. Language acquisition can be enhanced during summarizing by planning for students to talk about their summaries after they've applied the "keep, delete, and substitute" rules. The teacher will have repeatedly modeled the rule-based summarization strategy with think-alouds in which he or she keeps important information, deletes trivial and redundant material that is unnecessary to understanding, and substitutes one word for a list of words. Once students have attempted to repeat the same steps, they should share their summaries with partners or small groups. To frame the accountable student talk time, they can use sentence starters such as these:

- I selected this main idea . . .
- I picked these supporting details . . .
- I used these key words and phrases . . .

When students talk about the academic concept of summarizing, they're developing language in addition to content. Language becomes an action when students speak collaboratively with others. In the example sentence starters, students are not just using everyday conversational language; they are tapping into academic language about selecting main ideas, identifying supporting details, and using key words and phrases.

In the Common Core State Standards for mathematics, students are expected to make sense of problems and communicate about procedures related to problem solving—a key opportunity for developing oral academic language. The following 3rd grade math example illustrates how you can help students develop oral academic language while summarizing.

A 3rd grade math teacher can "go to the balcony" for the big-picture view of students engaged in talking about the content. The task could be multiplying a two-digit number by a one-digit number and summarizing the steps. While the teacher visualizes the multiplying or summarizing, he or she is also predicting exemplars—what the most proficient students would say; for example, "First, multiply the ones digit of the bottom number by the ones digit of the top number for 5 × 25." Next, the teacher determines the academic language that accompanies the math content by identifying the function of language and why students are conversing: to summarize. Finally, the teacher determines what students in the process of acquiring English need in order to engage in that level of academic talk:

- **Vocabulary:** *multiply, digit, product*
- **Grammar:** present tense, commands
- **Sentence starters:** First, ___. Next, _____. Then _____. Finally, _____.

By identifying the function of language along with the vocabulary, grammar, and sentence starters, the teacher is able to apply the academic language of this math task while simultaneously teaching content. Figure 8.2 illustrates the teacher's thinking.

FIGURE 8.2
Academic Language Framework for a 3rd Grade Math Lesson

Task	Exemplars	Academic Language			
		Function of Language	Vocabulary	Grammar	Sentence Starter(s)
Multiply a two-digit number by a one-digit number and summarize the steps.	"First, multiply the ones digit of the bottom number by the ones digit of the top number for 5 × 25."	summarizing	*multiply, digit, product*	present-tense, commands	First, ____. Next, _____. Then _____. Finally, _____.

Note Taking: Classroom Practice Recommendations

Note taking is closely related to summarizing because it requires students to take information and synthesize it using their own words. The purpose of note taking is to help students acquire and integrate knowledge; it is a way to organize and process information. Because culturally and linguistically diverse students are extracting new knowledge in a new language, they will need explicit instruction in the art of note taking.

The second edition of *Classroom Instruction That Works* proposes three classroom practices for taking notes:

- Give students teacher-prepared notes.
- Teach students a variety of note-taking formats.
- Provide opportunities for students to revise their notes and use them for review.

Give students teacher-prepared notes. Giving students teacher-prepared notes is a good introductory approach to note taking. Teacher-prepared notes are important because students acquiring English as another language learn from modeling. In this case, the teacher models for students how notes might be taken, providing a clear picture of what the teacher considers important.

A middle school science teacher wants students to understand basic facts about the parts of a frog and provides an example of teacher-prepared notes

(Figure 8.3). Besides being an exemplar of what the teacher considers to be the most salient points to record, the teacher also uses this type of note-taking format in the following ways:

- He provides Intermediate and Advanced Fluency students with written notes and asks students to add graphics.
- He provides notes with missing words for Speech Emergence and Early Production students and asks students to supply the missing words.
- He engages Preproduction students by asking them to point to parts of the teacher-prepared graphics (for example, "Point to where the frog hears.")

FIGURE 8.3
Teacher-Prepared Notes for English Language Learners

Teacher-Prepared Notes	Teacher-Prepared Graphics

I. Characteristics
 	
  A. Strong, webbed hind feet for leaping and swimming.
 	
  B. Hears through the tympanum.
 	
  C. Like humans, frogs' eyes come in various colors.
	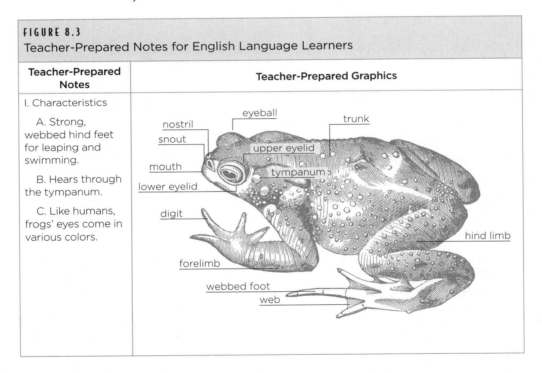

Teach students a variety of note-taking formats. Using a variety of note-taking formats can be beneficial to all students, not just emerging English users. We recommend the use of webbing, informal outlining, and combination notes. Webbing can be particularly helpful for students in the process of learning English, as it uses nonlinguistic representations (shapes, colors, and arrows) to show relationships among ideas. Webbing also offers students an opportunity to share their thinking, learn from their peers, and make corrections or additions (Stone & Urquhart, 2008), which can provide additional opportunities for developing oral academic language.

In addition to webbing, combination notes can be an effective format of note taking for English language learners because they combine both linguistic and nonlinguistic representations. By using combination notes, students acquiring English can record key ideas on the left side of a piece of paper and then draw or paste corresponding pictures on the right side. At the bottom of the note-taking page, students write a meaningful key idea. See Figure 8.4 for an example of combination notes.

FIGURE 8.4
Combination Notes Format for Note Taking

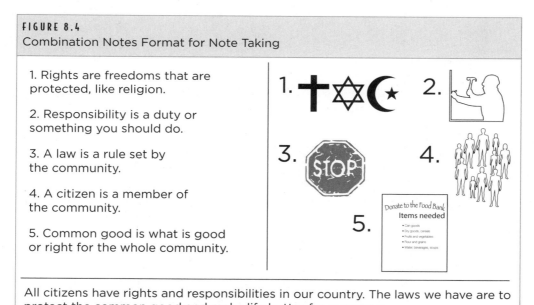

1. Rights are freedoms that are protected, like religion.

2. Responsibility is a duty or something you should do.

3. A law is a rule set by the community.

4. A citizen is a member of the community.

5. Common good is what is good or right for the whole community.

All citizens have rights and responsibilities in our country. The laws we have are to protect the common good and make life better for everyone.

Source: From *Classroom Instruction That Works, 2nd edition* (p. 96), by C. B. Dean, E. R. Hubbell, H. Pitler, and B. Stone, 2012, Alexandria, VA: ASCD. Copyright 2012 by McREL. Reprinted with permission.

Provide opportunities for students to revise their notes and use them for review. When we provide English language learners and others in need of language development with time to revise and review their notes, we open the door to language development. If students can review their notes in a structured academic conversation, then they can build their academic English.

Teachers implementing this recommendation can enhance it for English language learners and others in need of language development by making the review and revision process a part of accountable, productive academic talk time. Second-language learners will need explicit directions before they can engage in this process.

Example

> **Using Sentence Starters and Small-Group Work to Review Notes**
> **Grade Level:** Middle school
> **Strategy:** Foster academic language development during notes review.

A middle school teacher knows when his students are ready to review their notes and directs them to meet in pairs or small groups. He provides boundaries for the talk that should take place. He knows English language learners will have higher-level interactions using guidelines and sentence starters such as these:

- I identified this as important because . . .
- These are supporting details because . . .
- I took notes this way because . . .
- I heard the teacher say this is important . . .

As a format for review, the teacher focuses on having students repeat key concepts from class: "These are key concepts . . ." Note that all students, not just students acquiring English, will need direct instruction, followed by guided instruction in effective note-taking skills.

Using the Thinking Language Matrix

The Thinking Language Matrix can be used to include English-language-learning students at all levels in the note-taking process. Because note taking is a form of summarizing, students will again be working at a high level of thinking on Bloom's taxonomy—Synthesis. The example that follows explains how a teacher might use the process to create the completed matrix shown in Figure 8.5.

FIGURE 8.5
Thinking Language Matrix for Note Taking in 7th Grade Math

Levels of Thinking and Language Functions	Tiered Thinking Across Stages of Second-Language Acquisition				
Level of thinking and academic language required for any task; move from concrete recall to more complex, abstract levels.	Language moves from simple to complex in grammatical tenses, forms, vocabulary, etc.				
	WORD ⟶ MODEL ⟶ EXPAND ⟶ SOUND LIKE A BOOK				
	Preproduction: nonverbal response	**Early Production:** one-word response	**Speech Emergence:** phrases or short sentences	**Intermediate Fluency:** longer and more complex sentences	**Advanced Fluency:** near native
Synthesis arrange, assemble, collect, compose, construct, create, design, develop, formulate, manage, organize, plan, prepare, propose, set up	Students are provided with a completed notes template that contains the formulas and steps for solving the problems in words, as well as numerical examples. Students can use kinesthetic nonlinguistic representations to show the area and circumference of a circle. Manipulatives are available to support students in solving area and circumference problems.	Students are given the notes template with a word bank and examples that are out of order at the bottom of the page. As the teacher explains the formulas and how to use them, students select correct steps and examples from the bank to include in their notes. Students explain to partners the steps involved in solving the problem using sentence starters: First, I_____. Next, I _____.		Students are given a template to fill in as the teacher explains the formulas and how to use them. Students copy formulas and examples and create their own problems and solve them. Students explain their thinking to partners.	

Taking notes in a middle-level math class can be challenging for language learners. To support English language learners in her class, a 7th grade math teacher provides Preproduction students with notes she has prepared showing how to use the formulas for the area and circumference of a circle to solve problems. Early Production and Speech Emergence students receive a template with a word bank and examples to use as they complete their own notes.

Opportunities to develop oral academic language

As we have noted in other chapters, it is no longer just the English as a second language teacher who is charged with building a strong oral language base as a precursor to reading and writing. Classroom teachers with English language learners and others in need of language development are also becoming more aware of the need to systemically emphasize oral academic language development alongside content. The note-taking strategy provides a strategic means for accomplishing this undertaking.

When students work together, they learn from one another. Students new to the U.S. school system may not know what non–English language learners already innately know. Along with writing key information on the board, teachers can give the following cues for capturing main points:

- "You need to know this."
- "This is important."
- "Expect to see this on the test."

An informal cooperative learning structure could be used to give students occasions to talk with and learn from one another while reviewing their notes. For example, Paraphrase Passport is a speaking activity that could be used for reviewing content notes and building academic language (Kagan, 1992). Here is how it works:

- Students partner up as A and B.
- Partner A starts by saying, "I identified this as important because . . ."
- Partner B paraphrases what he or she heard: "What I think I heard you saying is . . ."
- Partner B contributes something from his or her notes: "I heard the teacher say this is important . . ."

- Partner A paraphrases what he or she heard Partner B say: "You think that . . ."
- The process continues until all notes have been reviewed.

Tips for Teaching Using Summarizing and Note Taking

- Remember that reciprocal teaching is a successful cooperative learning structure because it incorporates the key ingredient of positive interdependence: students depend on one another and cannot succeed alone. At the same time, when everyone has a role, individual accountability is addressed.
- If you rely on whole-class questions and answers for the four comprehension strategies involved in reciprocal teaching, culturally and linguistically diverse students may not raise their hands to contribute to the summary, ask questions, seek clarification, or make predictions. When group work is expected and everyone has a role, second-language learners will be engaged.
- Make sure that note taking engages students in processes that involve generating or synthesizing information. Avoid verbatim note taking.
- Encourage students to supplement their written note taking with nonlinguistic representations.
- Give students plenty of opportunities to review their notes with others. Doing so enables them to hear what others captured in their notes as being important.

9

Assigning Homework and Providing Practice

Assigning homework and providing practice gives students opportunities to expand their skills and practice what they've learned. Since the publication of the first edition of *Classroom Instruction That Works*, the research on homework and practice has been mixed. The impact of homework, in particular, on student achievement seems to be linked to the quality of the homework assigned, how assignments are monitored, the degree of parent support, and students' learning preferences (Hong, Milgram, & Rowell, 2004; Minotti, 2005). The research on practice suggests that standard practice (rereading text, for example) has little impact (McDaniel, Roediger, & McDermott, 2007), but overt practice (through the use of flash cards, for example) may be more effective.

Despite the mixed evidence, it's hard to imagine school without homework and practice, and when done right, both can positively affect student achievement. McREL's 2010 meta-analysis of literature on classroom practices found a small positive effect for assigning homework, with a larger effect for providing practice (Beesley & Apthorp, 2010).

Assigning Homework: Classroom Practice Recommendations

The second edition of *Classroom Instruction That Works* provides three recommendations for assigning homework:

- Develop and communicate a district or school homework policy.

- Design homework assignments that support academic learning and communicate their purpose.
- Provide feedback on assigned homework.

Develop and communicate a district or school homework policy. Homework policies should inform students and parents about the purpose of homework, estimate the amount of homework that students will typically receive, discuss consequences for not turning in assignments, and suggest ways in which parents can help. For students learning English, whenever possible, be sure to send this policy home in a language parents can understand.

In schools or classrooms with English language learners and others in need of language development, language objectives should be incorporated into homework, which may be a new concept for many people. Although homework in the content areas is typical, homework that involves oral academic language development is likely to be a different experience. Because academic language involves the vocabulary, grammar, and discourse of subject-matter instruction, homework in language development might focus on oral practice of those components.

In a school or classroom homework policy, it may be important to note that homework will not look the same for all students. As noted, homework for students learning English could contain language development practice, or their content homework may be modified with reduced complexity (such as a shortened list of science terms) or have an extended due date. Homework can also be differentiated based on students' level of second-language acquisition.

The following letter from a 4th grade teacher to all parents (also provided in parents' native languages) illustrates how you might communicate this idea:

Dear Parents,

The school day isn't long enough for students to finish all of the practice they need to become competent in all subjects. There will be homework each night so your child can reach proficiency. Each student has a planner for writing the homework assignment for each night. When the homework is completed, you will see a note from the teacher. Please check the planner each night.

If your child decides to work with another student on homework, do not be surprised if their homework is different. Not all students need the same practice in the same way.

Thank you,
Miss Thompson

Design homework assignments that support academic learning and communicate their purpose. When second-language learners are in mainstream classrooms, their homework assignments will vary depending on their level of language proficiency. All students should understand the purpose of each assignment. Homework has two purposes: some assignments may be for practicing or elaborating on vocabulary or other knowledge and skills already learned in school, whereas others will focus on preparing students for new information or will elaborate on information that has already been introduced.

Example

Differentiating Homework and Assignments for English Language Learners
Grade Level: 6
Strategy: Support students at all levels of language acquisition in an assignment to produce an information sheet.

Have you ever seen an English-language-learning student assigned the same homework as a non–English language learner? Is the second-language learner really practicing what he or she has learned, or is the student still struggling to learn the content (and associated academic language) and practicing the skill incorrectly?

In the following classroom assignment, a 6th grade science teacher wants students to show what they know about patterns of the environment by having them produce an information sheet or opinion paper on environmental issues related to Yellowstone National Park. The teacher considers the stages of second-language acquisition along with Bloom's taxonomy in this assignment to address the needs of students who are at introductory levels of learning and those who are ready for more abstract, analytical, in-depth, and advanced work:

- Preproduction and Early Production students can create an information sheet about an environmental issue related to Yellowstone using pictures and labels for things such as bison, lakes, mud snails, and fishermen.

- Speech Emergence and Intermediate Fluency students can create an information sheet about the causes and effects of environmental issues related to Yellowstone, such as aquatic invaders, bison management, or bio-prospecting.

- Advanced Fluency and native English speakers can write an opinion paper on policies related to Yellowstone's environment as it pertains to things such as water, animals, and land.

In addition to content homework and practice, the teacher assigns language homework or classroom practice. He knows that, at times, language may trump content because students acquiring English will need to reach a level of language proficiency in order to fully engage with the content. They need to practice speaking about the knowledge they are learning in the classroom and should be given opportunities to practice language structures accompanying subject matter.

In this lesson, Preproduction and Early Production students have crafted an information sheet on Yellowstone National Park's environmental issues, along with accompanying pictures and labels for singular and plural forms of the words *bison*, *lakes*, *mud snails*, and *fishermen*. Their homework assignment requires Preproduction and Early Production students to use the vocabulary of environmental issues in sentences using the stems "This is a _____. These are _____." For example, they verbalize: "This is a fisherman. These are fishermen. This is a lake. These are lakes." Just as students read aloud to improve their reading fluency, students acquiring a second language should speak aloud to become more fluent in English.

Provide feedback on assigned homework. Students acquiring English will benefit from a variety of feedback on their homework, from both their teachers and their peers. Peer feedback can be helpful for culturally and linguistically diverse students, provided that students are not inundated with advice from native-English-speaking students on how to correct every error. Emerging English users will also benefit from seeing examples of other students' homework and hearing the explanations provided.

Here are some suggestions for providing feedback before and after homework:

- Plan time to explain homework to English language learners.
- Explain both the task and its purpose.
- Show clear examples of expectations.
- Teach students to clarify and ask questions.
- Teach the "language of homework," such as (1) The (assignment) is due (date). (2) Practice (task) for _____ minutes. (3) Move the puzzle pieces while you say the words.

The 6th grade science teacher in the example has asked Preproduction and Early Production students to practice singular and plural forms of the words *bison*, *lakes*, *mud snails*, and *fishermen* with the sentence starters "This is a _____" and "These are _____." He notices that his students from Vietnam do not include the plural ending *s* when using the words during class time. Before providing feedback, the teacher contacts the English as a second language teacher and learns that the plural *s* is not a sound that transfers automatically, because two consonants do not occur together in Vietnamese. In other words, saying "lakes" and "snails" is difficult because each of those words already ends with a consonant sound orally, and for a speaker of Vietnamese, adding another consonant (a plural *s*) is unnatural and must be learned. After the English as a second language teacher has explicitly taught the students to produce the sound, more practice can be assigned as homework (using a mobile app such as GarageBand®, which allows for recording and playback), and specific feedback can be provided on the use of plural *s*.

Using the Thinking Language Matrix

The Thinking Language Matrix can be used to include students at all stages of English language acquisition in tiered homework and classroom assignments. In the Common Core State Standards for mathematics, students are expected to communicate about concepts.

In this example, 2nd grade students are asked to interpret data using pictographs. This activity falls into the Analysis level of Bloom's taxonomy. Students have been given a clear explanation of the purpose of this homework assignment: to practice what they have been learning about interpreting data. Not everyone receives the same assignment. All practice tasks are at the same level of Bloom's taxonomy but are differentiated based on the students' stages of second-language acquisition. Figure 9.1 shows how a teacher might use the language matrix to plan the homework assignments.

FIGURE 9.1
Thinking Language Matrix for Homework

Levels of Thinking and Language Functions	Tiered Thinking Across Stages of Second-Language Acquisition				
Level of thinking and academic language required for any task; move from concrete recall to more complex, abstract levels.	Language moves from simple to complex in grammatical tenses, forms, vocabulary, etc.				
	WORD ⟶ MODEL ⟶ EXPAND ⟶ SOUND LIKE A BOOK				
	Preproduction: nonverbal response	Early Production: one-word response	Speech Emergence: phrases or short sentences	Intermediate Fluency: longer and more complex sentences	Advanced Fluency: near native
Analysis analyze, appraise, calculate, categorize, compare, contrast, criticize, differentiate, discriminate, distinguish, examine, experiment, question, test	Students are given a partially completed graph. The teacher asks them to modify the graph (e.g., "Change the pictograph so it shows 15 dogs.").		Students are given a partially completed graph. The teacher asks them to modify the graph (e.g., "Change the pictograph so it shows 15 dogs."). Sentence starter: I added _____.	"There are 15 dogs in all because each dog symbol represents five dogs and there are three symbols." "There are five more dogs than cats because there is one more dog symbol."	

Opportunities to develop oral academic language

Homework provides an opportunity for students to practice oral language outside the classroom. Oral academic language applications can be incorporated into homework based on the homework's content. For example, using our Yellowstone homework assignment, a teacher can ask students to practice reading aloud the sentence stems developed to identify environmental concerns in Yellowstone National Park. It is not important if anyone else at home listens while the Preproduction/Early Production student practices aloud. Any language takes practice. These beginning-level students need to develop fluency in English, and homework requiring oral production meets this need. If a recording device can be used at home and returned to the teacher, then the teacher can give feedback to the student on fluency.

Providing Practice: Classroom Practice Recommendations

The second edition of *Classroom Instruction That Works* offers three ideas for providing practice:

- Clearly identify and communicate the purpose of practice activities.
- Design practice sessions that are short, focused, and distributed over time.
- Provide feedback on practice sessions.

Clearly identify and communicate the purpose of practice activities. Practice, like homework, needs to be aligned to the learning objectives (Dean et al., 2012). What is different about the concept of practice for English language learners? English language learners may need more oral practice than non–English language learners. In the *English Language Learner Resource Guide: Top Ten Instructional Tips for Schools with a Low Incidence of ELLs,* Hill and Hoak (2012) point out that teachers need to know the differences involved in teaching students who are acquiring English. To adjust literacy instruction for English language learners, Kauffman (2007) recommends more student interaction by engaging students in the use of academic language. When explaining a practice activity involving academic talk, teachers can convey to students that they are going to talk about what they are going to write before writing it; they are going to rehearse sounding like a book to improve their writing.

Example

Practicing Comparing and Contrasting

Grade Level: 6

Strategy: Compare and contrast essential elements in written and audiovisual text.

A 6th grade teacher wants students to learn to compare and contrast essential elements in written text and an audiovisual version of the same text. Using a text and a corresponding movie, she asks students to complete a Venn diagram and write about similarities and differences in the two forms of media. She is disappointed by the students' conclusions: "They're the same because they have the same plot." "They have the same characters." "They're different because one you read and one you see." When debriefing with this teacher, she returns to the lesson objective and the supports needed by English language learners and others in need of language development. For English language learners to practice using a Venn diagram, they must be given the characteristics or attributes for making the comparisons, they must have opportunities to hear similarities and differences from others, and they need practice time verbalizing similarities and differences before writing them.

The teacher tries the practice session again the next day. Using Numbered Heads Together (see Chapter 5), she asks each group to hear what each member has to say and then decide on one similarity and one difference between the written text and the film version based on how it makes them feel. When the groups report out, she hears comments such as these: "The movie made us feel sadder than the text because we saw Sarah crying." "The movie made us mad at her classmates because we could see her friends pointing and whispering behind her back, but we didn't pick that up in the book."

After each group reports out, she asks them to compare and contrast based on their degree of understanding. After the English language learners hear and verbalize similarities and differences for specific attributes and characteristics, she provides sentence stems for the written work and finds the scaffolding rewards her and her students with a better written product.

Design practice sessions that are short, focused, and distributed over time. Designing practice sessions that are short, focused, and distributed over time provides an opportunity for English-language-learning students to learn the language in addition to the content. When it comes to emerging English users, have you heard it said, "If you can't say it, you can't write it"? Educators from the Teaching Writing Center say it this way:

> The idea that "you learn to write by writing" is well and good for English-only students who need only to practice their writing skills to become better writers. However, this maxim is not helpful in describing the task for many ELLs. In this case, more writing is not the solution. Research suggests that more talking—oral language development—is the prerequisite to developing strong writing skills. (Williams, Stathis, & Gotsch, 2009, p. 21)

With an increasing amount of urgency being placed on reading and writing (Williams & Roberts, 2011), students are expected to practice writing throughout the day, during all subject areas. For culturally and linguistically diverse students and others in need of language development, good writing stems from good speaking. To improve written language output, provide multiple opportunities to practice rich academic talk. Students need to have something to write about. When students acquiring English as another language hear others talk about their ideas for writing, it serves as a stimulus for their own ideas. Talking before writing provides an oral base for the writing. Second-language-acquisition students can begin by writing what they have said. This conversational level of writing can be elevated to an academic level by teacher modeling—the teacher demonstrates how talking and writing are connected—as follows:

- Students have an experience.

- The teacher asks students to describe the experience, and the teacher writes what they say.
- Students read their own words.
- The teacher shows how to make those sentences sound like a book based on particular skills such as combining sentences, inserting transition words, and using higher-level vocabulary words.

The following example represents a short and focused practice time for writing. This focused practice on how to shift from conversational language to academic language targets a specific aspect of writing.

Example

Focused Practice Using Academic Language
Grade Level: 3
Strategy: Practice transition words.

Students in Ms. Young's 3rd grade class are reading an informational text about China. Periodically, they stop and rephrase what they read. To elevate the classroom talk, Ms. Young scaffolds the development and use of academic language by helping her students use the transition words *first*, *next*, and *furthermore* in their paraphrasing. Laminated sentence starters with the transition words are in front of the students, and the teacher completes those sentences while students verbalize. The teacher plans to use these transition words in writing to accompany what students are reading every day for the first week, every other day for the following week, and once a week for subsequent weeks until students begin to use transition words in their independent writing.

Provide feedback on practice sessions. Providing feedback on practice can help students understand what they're doing correctly—and what they're not. For English language learners, teachers can provide feedback on the acquisition of English by using the Word-MES formula detailed in Chapter 3:

1. Provide feedback on **word** selection with Preproduction students.

2. Model for Early Production students.
3. Expand what Speech Emergence students have said.
4. Help Intermediate and Advanced Fluency students "sound like a book."

Example

> **Providing Feedback Using Word-MES**
> **Grade Level:** K
> **Strategy:** Provide feedback to students retelling a story.

A kindergarten teacher wants to provide feedback to students retelling *The Three Little Pigs*. In a small group with Preproduction students who sequence pictures for the story, she gives feedback on the words they use, and she helps them say words such as *wolf*, *pig*, *house*, *straw*, *bricks*, and *blow*.

With Early Production students, she models. When a student says, "wolf blowed," the teacher models, "Yes, the wolf *blew* and *blew*." The teacher helps Speech Emergence students expand oral sentences. When a student says, "He blew the house down," the teacher responds, "Yes, he blew the *straw* house down." For Intermediate and Advanced Fluency students, the teacher helps them sound like a book by exposing them to academic vocabulary. Students can retell *The Three Little Pigs* using synonyms for the word *bad* in "big, bad wolf."

TRY THIS: Before requiring students to write, provide a structure for small-group talk.

If you are asking students to write a journal entry, first set up Paraphrase Passport (see Chapter 8). As students talk back and forth with their partners, English language learners hear examples of what could be written, and they have an opportunity to practice composing sentences orally before beginning a journal entry.

Using the Thinking Language Matrix

We can use the Thinking Language Matrix to plan for students acquiring English and others in need of language development to practice language that appears in academic content. The Common Core State Standards for language arts and literacy in history/social studies require 5th grade students to read informational text and write informative/explanatory texts to examine a topic. They must convey ideas and information, clearly linking ideas within and across categories of information using words, phrases, and clauses (e.g., *by contrast, especially*).

As students plan for writing, they should talk first. In the example described here, the teacher facilitates talk that supports written language when expecting students to compare (an Application task in Bloom's taxonomy) two or more world religions. The example explains how a teacher might create the completed matrix shown in Figure 9.2.

FIGURE 9.2
Thinking Language Matrix for Comparing and Contrasting World Religions

Levels of Thinking and Language Functions	Tiered Thinking Across Stages of Second-Language Acquisition				
	Language moves from simple to complex in grammatical tenses, forms, vocabulary, etc.				
Level of thinking and academic language required for any task; move from concrete recall to more complex, abstract levels.	WORD ⟶ MODEL ⟶ EXPAND ⟶ SOUND LIKE A BOOK				
	Preproduction: nonverbal response	**Early Production:** one-word response	**Speech Emergence:** phrases or short sentences	**Intermediate Fluency:** longer and more complex sentences	**Advanced Fluency:** near native
Analysis analyze, appraise, calculate, categorize, compare, contrast, criticize, differentiate, discriminate, distinguish, examine, experiment, question, test	Students are asked to locate Israel and Mecca on a map.	Sentence frames: _____ and _____ are similar because _____. _____ and _____ are dissimilar because _____.		"Based on where they were founded, Judaism and Christianity are similar because they were both founded in Israel. By contrast, Islam is dissimilar from Judaism and Christianity because Islam was founded in Mecca."	

In 5th grade social studies, the students in Taipei American School compared world religions by using a comparison matrix. The first step was facilitating students talking with other students to compare and contrast world religions based on various characteristics, such as where the religion was founded and who the founder was. Next, the teacher built in the use of academic language by requiring students to use the words *similar* and *dissimilar*. She then further increased the use of content-related academic language by showing students how to use adverbial clauses with the words *although* and *even though*. The teacher planned for students to practice verbalizing their similarities and differences with *similar/dissimilar* and adverbial clauses for short, focused practice sessions that were distributed over time until these language traits appeared in their writing.

Opportunities to develop oral academic language

We have all heard the idiom "practice makes perfect." Students learning English need dual practice because they are learning a new language and new content. To practice the English language, they need to speak the English language with one another and with non–English language learners. Again, this is not about practicing conversational English. Practicing rich oral academic language is the goal because it will serve as a foundation for literacy.

The experts on the National Literacy Panel on Language—Minority Children and Youth also recognize the need to practice talking: "Instruction in the key components of reading is necessary—but not sufficient—for teaching language minority students to read and write proficiently in English. Oral proficiency in English is critical . . . but student performance suggests that it is often overlooked" (August & Shanahan, 2006, p. 4).

Tips for Teaching Using Homework and Practice

- Remember the two reasons for homework: to practice or elaborate on what's been learned and to prepare for new, upcoming information. Students learning English need to have what they learn reinforced so they don't spend time practicing something in error because they haven't learned the content yet.

- Homework assignments can cover language development or content, or both. Sometimes, learning the language of the subject matter should be the priority. For example, to prepare for a new unit, students acquiring English may need exposure to the new vocabulary before encountering those words in a text.

- Whenever you're thinking about asking the whole class questions, reconsider and arrange for small groups or partners to discuss possible answers. It will take only a minute or two for partners to confer over a question you pose. By contrast, if you ask the whole class a question and only one student answers, it will take a significant chunk of time to ask additional questions so that each student gets a chance to respond.

- After purposefully planning for students to be engaged with other students orally, ask yourself if they are using conversational language or academic language. As a guideline, remember that academic language consists of longer, more complex sentences with high-level vocabulary; students sound like a book.

Part III

Helping Students Extend and Apply Knowledge

10

Identifying Similarities and Differences

When we identify similarities and differences, we compare information, sort concepts into categories, and make connections to existing knowledge—in other words, we're making sense of the world (Dean et al., 2012). The second edition of *Classroom Instruction That Works* presents four strategies in this category and defines them as follows:

- **Comparing** is the process of identifying similarities between or among things or ideas. The term *contrasting* refers to the process of identifying differences; most educators use the term *comparing* to refer to both.
- **Classifying** is the process of organizing things into groups and labeling them according to their similarities.
- **Creating metaphors** is the process of identifying a general topic or basic pattern in a specific topic and then finding another topic that appears to be quite different but has the same general pattern.
- **Creating analogies** is the process of identifying relationships between pairs of concepts—identifying relationships between relationships.

These four strategies "help move students from existing knowledge to new knowledge, concrete to abstract, and separate to connected ideas" (Dean et al., 2012, p. 119). This progression can be particularly important for students acquiring English as another language, because, as we've noted, a lack of language ability is not equivalent to an inability to think at high levels.

Identifying Similarities and Differences: Classroom Practice Recommendations

The second edition of *Classroom Instruction That Works* offers the following recommendations for classroom practice:

- Teach students a variety of ways to identify similarities and differences.
- Guide students as they engage in the process of identifying similarities and differences.
- Provide supporting cues to help students identify similarities and differences.

Teach students a variety of ways to identify similarities and differences. When we address higher-order thinking functions, such as identifying similarities and differences, it's important to teach students the process explicitly, ideally using content with which students are already familiar. Many English language learners will benefit from orally identifying similarities and differences, which also provides an opportunity to develop oral academic language. Attribute charts, which can be adapted according to the content being taught, provide one way to help second-language learners and other students in need of language development build and review the vocabulary needed for identifying similarities and differences. (See Figure 10.1 for an example.) Attribute charts allow Preproduction students to build vocabulary, Early Production students to use familiar vocabulary, and Speech Emergence students to practice using sentences. Intermediate and Advanced Fluency students can use attribute charts to work on improving their academic language knowledge by using words other than *same* and *different* as they compare items.

Students need to understand the concept of attributes and characteristics before they identify similarities through comparing, classifying, creating metaphors, or creating analogies, because each of these strategies relies on identifying the distinguishing characteristics of items and ideas. Once teachers have reviewed the attribute chart with students, they can guide students through the strategies themselves.

Comparing

The first strategy, comparing, is a three-step process:

1. Select the items you want to compare.

FIGURE 10.1
Attribute Chart

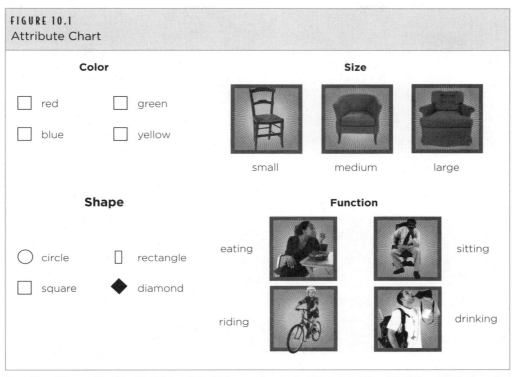

Source: From *Classroom Instruction That Works with English Language Learners* (p. 104), by J. D. Hill and K. M. Flynn, 2006, Alexandria, VA: ASCD. Copyright 2006 by McREL. Reprinted with permission.

2. Identify characteristics of the items on which to base your comparison.
3. Explain how the items are similar to and different from one another with respect to the characteristics you selected.

Example

Comparing and Contrasting for Linguistically Diverse Students
Grade Level: 1
Strategy: Help students become proficient in comparing and contrasting.

A 1st grade teacher wants his students to become proficient at comparing and contrasting. To scaffold learning for culturally and linguistically diverse students and others in need of language development, this teacher begins with the familiar, providing sentence starters and modeling the process.

He uses a think-aloud to model the steps: "I have two things to compare: a pen and a pencil. First, let's talk about color. The pencil and the pen are different because the pencil is yellow and the pen is gray. Next, let's talk about size. The pencil and the pen are the same because they are both small. Now, let's talk about shape. The pencil and the pen are the same because they are both long and round. Finally, let's talk about function. The pencil and the pen are the same because both are used for writing."

Next, the teacher provides guided practice, asking students to complete his sentence: "Let's talk about color. The pencil and the pen are different because . . ." After steering his students through this whole-class practice, he places them in groups of four so they can compare and contrast using the sentence starters and any two objects of their choice.

For students learning English, it can be helpful to use nonlinguistic representations, posted on chart paper, to illustrate the various attributes of each object as you model the process. What are the objects made from? If we go back to our pencil and pen example, representations might include plastic and wood. Once you've modeled the process, ask students to select two common classroom items to compare. Then, have them use the sentence starters to review and discuss each attribute.

A common mistake during this process is skipping Step 2—identifying characteristics on which to base the comparison—and progressing straight from selecting items for comparison to explaining how the objects are similar to and different from each other. Especially for students acquiring English, however, Step 2 provides a valuable opportunity to work on vocabulary and oral language development. As students become more proficient at using the attribute chart to identify characteristics, you can continue to move from the basic (e.g., color, size, shape, and function, when comparing items) to the academic (e.g., inventions, agriculture, and religion, when comparing civilizations).

Classifying

The attribute chart can also be used when classifying, the second strategy in identifying similarities and differences. The classifying process has seven steps:

1. Identify the items you want to classify.
2. Select an item, describe its key attributes, and identify other items that have the same attributes.
3. Create a category by specifying the attributes that items must have for membership in this category.
4. Select another item, describe its key attributes, and identify other items that have the same attributes.
5. Create a second category by specifying the attributes that items must have for membership in the category.
6. Repeat the previous two steps until all items are classified and the specific attributes have been identified for membership in each category.
7. If necessary, combine categories or split them into smaller categories, and specify attributes that determine membership in each category.

Again, just as with comparing, scaffold students' learning by starting with familiar, basic attributes in each category before moving toward more rigorous academic attributes.

Example

Classifying by Theme
Grade Level: Middle school
Strategy: Focus on basic attributes of familiar objects to learn how to classify.

A middle school teacher helps students learn about classifying by starting with items in the classroom. For students acquiring English as another language, this activity provides an opportunity to focus on basic attributes of familiar objects. Applying the task of classifying to a more academic task, the students then organize books in their classroom library according to themes. They start by using the physical books themselves, with pictures to represent the themes; then they classify the books by using the book titles and words for the themes without the pictorial support.

Creating metaphors

Figurative language, the type of language used in metaphors, can present a particular challenge for emerging English users. As Kathpalia and Carmel (2011) note, instruction for most English language learners focuses on improving "grammatical competence," with little attention paid to "metaphorical competence" (p. 274). However, metaphors can help students access—or understand—information, process information, and apply it to their own lives (Wormeli, 2009), making them a valuable tool for encouraging higher-order thinking.

Creating metaphors involves three steps:

1. Identify the basic or most important elements of the information or situation with which you are working.
2. Write the basic information as a more general pattern by replacing words for specific things with words for more general things and by summarizing information whenever possible.
3. Find new information or situations to which the general pattern applies.

A high school teacher adapted this strategy for students acquiring English by reducing the linguistic complexity and adding pictures, as follows:

1. Select something to describe (example: *a coworker*).

2. Think of ways to describe it (example: *active, energetic, fun*).

3. Select one of the descriptors (example: *active*).

4. Find something else that fits this description, based on something familiar (example: *volcano*).

5. Create the metaphor: *The coworker is a volcano.*

Creating analogies

Analogies express the relationship between two pairs of items; for example, "puppy is to dog as kitten is to cat." Analogies can be challenging for all students, not just second-language-acquisition students, because they involve relationships between relationships (Dean et al., 2012). Analogies, like metaphors, can help activate background knowledge and encourage students to make connections to what they already know. For students acquiring English, we talk about how important it is to activate and access their prior knowledge. We do this to make connections to students' background knowledge and to what is familiar to them based on their life experiences. Analogies can be a tool for achieving this.

For example, part/whole analogies can be used when practicing and reviewing what's been learned in science on the study of human body systems. The content objective is to understand that there are different systems within the body that work independently and together to form a functioning human body. The academic language of this content could focus on using analogous language to review systems.

The second edition of *Classroom Instruction That Works* presents three steps for creating an analogy:

1. Identify how the two items in the first pair are related.
2. State the relationship in a general way.
3. Identify another pair of items that share a similar relationship.

Example

> **Creating Analogies with Linguistically Diverse Students**
> **Grade Level: 5**
> **Strategy:** Provide support for students to understand the structure of analogies.

A 5th grade teacher wants to implement analogies for understanding functions of the human body. To use the three steps with culturally and linguistically diverse students and others in need of language development, he provides examples of analogies that reflect the relationship between the object and its function or purpose:

pen : write

fork : _____

He shares how we traditionally verbalize analogies by saying, "*Pen* is to *write* as *fork* is to *eat*. We're not going to say it that way for a while. We are going to replace the words *is to* with the relationship words *used for*: A pen is used for writing, and a fork is used for eating." Once students become familiar with this type of analogy, they can use it for reviewing science terms:

lungs : breathing

kidneys : _____

"The lungs are used for breathing. The kidneys are used for filtering."

Analogies can make new and unfamiliar concepts more meaningful to students by connecting what they already know to what they are learning. The next step is to involve students in creating their own analogies. When students create their own analogies for new concepts, the analogy can provide a way to assess their understanding of the new concepts.

Guide students as they engage in the process of identifying similarities and differences. When we adapt this strategy for English language learners and others in need of language development, we add a step: Guide students as they engage in *and discuss* the process of identifying similarities and differences. This classroom practice offers a number of opportunities for teachers to help emerging English users and others in need of language development use, practice, and reinforce language. For example, when guiding students through an attribute chart such as the one in Figure 10.1, teachers can begin by modeling sentence starters and then guiding students to discuss attributes of two objects with their classmates, using the sentence starters. Classifying is also primarily a teacher-directed activity with a gradual release of responsibility to students, who then form their own classifications and talk about them with their peers.

The following example illustrates how we might guide students to create and discuss metaphors and analogies during an elementary-level literacy lesson. As teachers, if we want students to grasp a new concept, then we need to become more strategic at helping them picture it. If we want to help students make sense of information, then we can have them create a metaphor by connecting what they don't know to what they already know.

Example

Creating Metaphors
Grade Level: Elementary
Strategy: Connect background knowledge to new content.

For this activity, the teacher directs and guides students to create a metaphor, as follows:

1. Select something to describe: *trees*
2. Think of ways to describe trees: *big, alive, beautiful*
3. Select one of the descriptors: *big*

4. Find something else that is big but is based on something familiar: *giants*

5. Metaphor: *Trees are giants*.

Alternatively, the teacher uses a T-chart graphic organizer to guide students in creating an analogy, as follows:

1. Place the word and pictorial representation of trees in the left-hand column, and ask students to discuss and list everything they know about trees in that column.

2. Second, ask students to place a picture of a giant in the right-hand column of the T-chart and discuss and list everything they know about giants in that column.

3. Students talk through and write as many connections as possible, using the sentence starter "Trees are like giants because _____." "Trees are like giants because they are both very big."

4. Students create a product or nonlinguistic representation that demonstrates or explains the key concepts.

Provide supporting cues to help students identify similarities and differences. You can use an attribute chart as a resource for providing supporting cues when you first begin using this strategy. Eventually, we want students to make rigorous comparisons, so the attribute chart can be used to extensively model for students how to identify items and characteristics that are meaningful and interesting and to provide students with feedback about how well they do. After practicing with the familiar, teachers then move students to the academic. Some of the attributes to be added for comparing characters in a story include, for example, personality and motivation. If the items and characteristics are not meaningful, students will not make new distinctions or come to new conclusions about the targeted knowledge.

Make sure students understand that the purpose of doing a comparison is to extend and refine their understanding of what they're learning. Asking students to select different characteristics to compare will help them move beyond the obvious.

Example

> **Begin with the Familiar**
> **Grade Level:** Middle school
> **Strategy:** Help students understand how to compare and contrast.

A middle school math teacher wants students to compare and contrast polygons. First, they practice with two classroom items and an attribute chart. Partners are instructed to compare and contrast their shoes based on color, size, composition, and parts. After practicing with the basic attributes and familiar items, the teacher moves into the academic area of math. The math attribute chart contains characteristics such as angles and surfaces. Referring to the chart when comparing and contrasting polygons, students make statements such as "The hexagon has more angles than the rectangle."

TRY THIS: Engage students in identifying metaphors.

Play one of your students' favorite pop songs that contains metaphors, and provide the lyrics. Begin by pointing out one of the metaphors, using a think-aloud about how the two items being described are similar. After conducting some guided practice, place students into small groups so they can collaborate on finding and describing metaphors. For independent practice, students can bring in favorite songs and identify and explain the meanings of the songs' metaphors.

Using the Thinking Language Matrix

The Thinking Language Matrix can be used to help English-language-learning students at all levels of language acquisition identify similarities and differences. The strategies of comparing and categorizing fall under the Analysis level of Bloom's taxonomy. The example that follows explains how a teacher might create the completed matrix shown in Figure 10.2.

In this example, students in a kindergarten class are playing a classifying memory game. Using pictures of different habitats and face-down cards of animal pictures, students are told to take turns turning over two cards. To make a match, both cards must have pictures of animals that live in the same place—on a farm, inside a home as a pet, in the jungle, or in the desert. Preproduction students use pictures to confirm a match and place the cards in the proper environment. For the match to count, Early Production and Speech Emergence students must explain why the two cards are the same, using the sentence frame

---

FIGURE 10.2
Thinking Language Matrix for a Classifying Memory Game

Levels of Thinking and Language Functions	Tiered Thinking Across Stages of Second-Language Acquisition				
Level of thinking and academic language required for any task; move from concrete recall to more complex, abstract levels.	Language moves from simple to complex in grammatical tenses, forms, vocabulary, etc.				
	WORD ⟶ MODEL ⟶ EXPAND ⟶ SOUND LIKE A BOOK				
	Preproduction: nonverbal response	**Early Production:** one-word response	**Speech Emergence:** phrases or short sentences	**Intermediate Fluency:** longer and more complex sentences	**Advanced Fluency:** near native
Analysis analyze, appraise, calculate, cat-egorize, compare, contrast, criticize, differentiate, dis-criminate, distin-guish, examine, experiment, ques-tion, test	Students are provided with pictures of all of the habitats and face-down cards that dis-play the names and pictures of animals. Students turn over cards and place them in the correct habi-tat. If both cards are in the same habi-tat, then they have a match.	Sentence starter: The _____ and the _____ both live_____. Students choose from a word bank that includes animals' names and habitats.		"The cow and the goat both live on a farm."	

"The ___ and the ___ both live ____" and a word bank of animal names and habitats. Students can also explain why two cards are not a match, using the sentence frame "The ____ lives _____, and the _____ lives ___." The same word bank can be used to complete this sentence. Intermediate and Advanced Fluency students no longer need the supports provided by sentence starters and word banks and should be expected to verbalize in complete sentences.

Opportunities to develop oral academic language

Identifying similarities and differences provides abundant opportunities for developing oral academic language, particularly when using the strategy of creating analogies. For English language learners and others in need of language development, it is important to be aware of how to verbalize analogies. For example, native English speakers might typically say, "Chair is to sit as bike is to ride." However, for second-language learners and others in need of language development, we need to take out the words *is to* and verbalize the type of analogy instead. For example, a chair is *used* for sitting, and a bike is *used* for riding.

When guiding, start with the familiar and scaffold for culturally and linguistically diverse students and others in need of language development, not only by verbalizing the type of analogy when orally "reading" the analogy but also by showing the different elements to add or subtract when students design analogies. We can provide the most scaffolding by removing only one element from the analogy—for example, "A leg is part of a chair; a steering wheel is part of a ____." We can increase the complexity by increasing the number of missing elements:

Two missing elements: A leg is part of a chair; the ____ is part of a ____.

Four missing elements: A ____ is part of a ____; the ____ is part of a ____.

In the Next Generation Science Standards, students are expected to construct explanations and communicate ideas, concepts, and information related to a phenomenon or system (natural or designed). The following example (see Figure 10.3) illustrates how a teacher has addressed oral language development while comparing and contrasting.

FIGURE 10.3
Academic Language Framework for an 8th Grade Science Task

Task	Exemplars	Academic Language			
		Function of Language	Vocabulary	Grammar	Sentence Starter(s)
Compare and contrast elements, compounds, and mixtures.	"Water is a compound because two or more elements have chemically combined."	comparing and contrasting	*substance, element, compound, mixture, chemical, physical, break/broken, combine*	comparatives, irregular verbs	Water is a _____ because it can/cannot be broken down into a simpler substance.

First, the teacher "goes to the balcony" and looks down on her 8th grade class while they're comparing and contrasting elements, compounds, and mixtures. The teacher records this task in the Task area of the template. Next, the teacher identifies the language function words associated with the task and records them in the Function of Language portion of the template. In this 8th grade science example, the function of language is *compare and contrast*.

Then the teacher writes down what she expects students to say as they engage in discussion. What rich oral academic language would they use as they engage with one another to discuss, explain, and compare? She records one or two examples in the Exemplars section. In 8th grade, proficient speakers could be expected to say, "Elements are pure substances that cannot be broken down by chemical or physical means. *X* is an element because it cannot be broken down into a simpler substance."

Finally, she decides what students acquiring English need in order to engage at that level of academic talk. She records these items in the appropriate parts of the template: Vocabulary, Grammar, and Sentence Starter(s). By identifying the function of language along with the vocabulary, grammar, and sentence starters, the teacher is able to address the language implications of this science task while simultaneously teaching content.

Tips for Teaching Using Identifying Similarities and Differences

- When working with analogies, start with teacher-directed analogies and gradually transition to student-generated analogies.
- In addition to using an attribute chart for common analogies, ask students to look for subject-specific analogies throughout the day and list the types discovered. Examples include opposites (graceful and clumsy), location (Denmark and Europe), and part-to-whole relationships (femur and leg). Students acquiring English will also benefit from access to pictures to accompany the analogies.
- Increase students' use of academic vocabulary by creating activities for verbalizing content vocabulary when classifying, comparing, and creating metaphors and analogies.
- To teach the syntax of the content, help students learn how to shape and use adverbial clauses. For example, when explaining similarities and differences, use clauses with *although* and *even though*.
- When addressing the discourse of subject matter, plan for abundant opportunities for students to talk so they can practice, review, and apply what they've been learning by verbalizing their thinking process while crafting comparisons and contrasts using classifying, comparing, metaphors, and analogies.
- Allow for plenty of talk time so students can demonstrate their verbal abilities before moving them into written forms of distinguishing similarities and differences.

11

Generating and Testing Hypotheses

When we hear the phrase "generating and testing hypotheses," our minds naturally jump to science; we think of laboratories, test tubes, and people in white coats. However, science does not have an exclusive claim on this instructional strategy, which engages students in complex reasoning that can be used in other content areas.

The process of generating and testing hypotheses requires English language learners to access prior knowledge, apply new knowledge, and explain their conclusions. Any time we use "if . . . then" reasoning, we enter the realm of generating and testing hypotheses. (For example, when studying transportation, we might ask students what would happen if they had to travel by train rather than by car.)

Berman, Minicucci, McLaughlin, Nelson, and Woodworth (1995) write about the need to create new classroom environments that help students learning English acquire higher-level language and reasoning skills. They also note that these students do not always have full access to middle school science and math classes, where inductive and deductive reasoning are generally taught. With that in mind, it is particularly important not to wait for middle school science and mathematics classes to introduce students to inductive and deductive reasoning.

Generating and Testing Hypotheses: Classroom Practice Recommendations

The second edition of *Classroom Instruction That Works* has two recommendations for classroom practice:

- Engage students in a variety of structured tasks for generating and testing hypotheses.
- Ask students to explain their hypotheses and their conclusions.

Engage students in a variety of structured tasks for generating and testing hypotheses. A variety of tasks can provide a context for generating and testing hypotheses. These tasks include systems analysis, problem solving, experimental inquiry, and investigation. In systems analysis, students analyze the parts of a system and how they interact. Problem solving focuses on troubleshooting and overcoming limitations to achieve goals. During experimental inquiry, students generate and test explanations of observed phenomena. Finally, investigation involves students in the process of resolving contradictions in past events.

Second-language-acquisition students can participate in generating and testing hypotheses in a mainstream classroom, but language complexity must be reduced. For example, you may want to assign Preproduction students to any part of the process that requires hands-on creativity. They should also note new vocabulary in notebooks and create visuals to associate with the words. Early Production students will do well with manipulatives and opportunities that allow them to practice the vocabulary of the lesson. Speech Emergence students will understand the task at hand and be able to communicate in short sentences. Intermediate and Advanced Fluency students will be participating at nearly the same level as English-dominant students.

Let's look at a systems analysis example from the second edition of *Classroom Instruction That Works* and then consider how we can adapt it for English language learners.

Example

> **Analyzing How Parts of a System Interact**
> **Grade Level:** High school
> **Strategy:** Use a simulation to help students understand the collapse of the housing market.

Mr. Jonas, a high school social studies teacher, wants to show how various practices led to the collapse of the housing market during the recession of the late 2000s. To demonstrate, he sets up a two-day simulation in which students "sell" their desks to peers who easily qualify for loans much larger than they can actually afford. The students who clean up their desks and move them to the sunny side of the room of the room enjoy seeing that they can charge much more for their desks than other students can charge.

Midway through the simulation, Mr. Jonas informs some of the students that they have lost their jobs and can no longer continue making mortgage payments to the bank. The class quickly realizes that the banks are no longer able to give loans, since they aren't getting paid by lenders. Some students realize that they overpaid for a simple desk.

Mr. Jonas asks students to form groups of three and identify different parts of the economic system and how they interacted in the simulation. He also challenges students to propose a change in one part of the system and predict what might happen to the other parts of the system if that change were made. Using this simulation, Mr. Jonas helps his students see how a few changes to an economic system can wreak havoc on the system as a whole.

Simulation, as in the example just presented, is an effective support for English language learners. Rather than reading about economic collapse, students are acting it out. For students in need of language development, Mr. Jonas will want to preteach major concepts and vocabulary such as *collapse, housing market, loans,* and *mortgage payment*s. To additionally support language learners, he can provide hands-on materials such as "For Sale" signs with dollar amounts and "money" to borrow from the bank to pay desk owners and use for mortgage payments. When students are required to change one element of the system and make predictions, English language learners will benefit from sentence frames such as "If we change _____, then _____ will happen."

Ask students to explain their hypotheses and their conclusions. By now, you'll recognize that this recommendation provides a clear opportunity for students to practice oral academic language. Again, to intentionally provide language instruction along with content, we need to create a planned time for students to talk. In Chapter 5, we provided specific cooperative learning structures that facilitate student talk time. Of course, students aren't just talking for the sake of talking. The purpose of the exchange is to increase English language acquisition and move students through the stages of language learning until they reach a stage in which they have enough English to perform as competently as non–English language learners. Remember, talking isn't an end in itself; the rationale for talking is to develop the language of the classroom, which is necessary to perform well on tests and write competently.

Once you have selected a time for students to talk in an informal cooperative learning structure, the next step is to determine language function and structure (see Chapter 3). In determining language function, you acknowledge the reason that students are talking: to sequence, explain, or persuade. Next, project what you would like to hear students say in their explanation of the hypothesis or conclusion; in other words, establish an exemplar. Now ask yourself, "What will second-language-acquisition students need in order to participate at that level of talk?" Specifically, think in terms of sentence starters, key vocabulary, and grammatical structures. Supply what students in the process of acquiring English will need to be orally successful.

Example

Decision Making
Grade Level: High school
Strategy: Use decision making to determine a solution to a specific problem.

A high school physics teacher wants students to use decision making to determine a solution to meet a specific need. He knows that his English language learners will not benefit from a lecture as much as they will learn through a problem-based approach. Before beginning the hands-on experience, he preteaches the following vocabulary terms for explaining their hypotheses and conclusions: *invention, weight distribution, columns, cylinders*.

Next, he organizes table teams composed of mixed groups of English language learners and non–English language learners. He provides direction using the materials at hand:

You are going to create an invention that is at least two inches tall (shows on ruler) and will be able to sustain the weight of four physics books (demonstrates by supporting four books with hands) for at least 30 seconds (shows with clock). The more weight the invention holds (points to more books), the better. You may use only one half-sheet of construction paper (points to displays) and two inches of masking tape (points to displays).

Take five minutes to brainstorm ideas and hypothesize the likelihood that your invention will work using the sentence stem "If we try _____, then _____ will happen." After brainstorming, test your hypotheses and discuss what revisions might be necessary to meet the set conditions. A note taker will be assigned to record ideas and discussion topics.

Using the Thinking Language Matrix

The Thinking Language Matrix can be used to include English language learners at all levels of language acquisition in generating and testing hypotheses. One of the structured tasks included in the recommendation to engage students in a variety of structured tasks for generating and testing hypotheses is investigation. This task involves identifying and resolving issues regarding past events about which there are confusions or contradictions. We are asking students to argue and defend, which are examples of Evaluation on Bloom's taxonomy. The example that follows explains how a teacher might create the completed matrix shown in Figure 11.1.

TRY THIS: Remind students to sound like scientists when explaining their hypotheses and conclusions.

When students are reporting on their hypotheses and conclusions, listen for signs of academic language: longer, more complex sentences and a higher-level vocabulary. When the opportunity presents itself, reorganize two simple sentences into a longer, more complex sentence with a conjunction or dependent clause, or ask students to restate a conclusion using less frequently used vocabulary. As English language learners hear academic language, they will venture into using it as well.

FIGURE 11.1
Thinking Language Matrix for Clarifying Different Points of View

Levels of Thinking and Language Functions	Tiered Thinking Across Stages of Second-Language Acquisition				
Level of thinking and academic language required for any task; move from concrete recall to more complex, abstract levels	Language moves from simple to complex in grammatical tenses, forms, vocabulary, etc.				
	WORD ⟶ MODEL ⟶ EXPAND ⟶ SOUND LIKE A BOOK				
	Preproduction: nonverbal response	**Early Production:** one-word response	**Speech Emergence:** phrases or short sentences	**Intermediate Fluency:** longer and more complex sentences	**Advanced Fluency:** near native
Evaluation appraise, argue, assess, attach, choose, compare, defend, estimate, evaluate, judge, predict, rate, select, support, value	Students are given a series of pictures that show events related to the European "discovery" of America, and they need to arrange them in a sequence that expresses their opinion.	Sentence starter: I _____ that Christopher Columbus discovered America because _____.		"I disagree that Christopher Columbus discovered America because there were many people on the continent before he arrived."	

An 8th grade social studies teacher decides to use the task of investigation to help students clarify different points of view about the same historical event. As students learn about exploration, the teacher provides them with two articles to read and consider regarding the European "discovery" of America. One article suggests that Christopher Columbus discovered America. The opposing perspective is represented in an article in which Native Americans dispute Columbus's discovery. The teacher implements the Four Corners activity (see Chapter 5) to provide students with an opportunity to discuss their perspectives with other students, both in their group and in other groups with opposing views. The teacher considers the language that will be needed to engage in this informal cooperative learning structure and provides a range of supports based on the students' stages of English language acquisition.

Opportunities to develop oral academic language

When we explain something, we make that thing—an idea, a situation, or a problem—clear to someone else by describing it in more detail or revealing relevant facts or ideas. The act of explaining naturally lends itself to student-to-student interaction. Many teachers are already deliberate in including reading and writing in all content areas. As the Common Core State Standards and the Next Generation Science Standards are implemented, teachers will need to address linguistic and subject-matter needs (Understanding Language, n.d.). In other words, it's time for educators to start thinking about how to be more strategic in delivering purposeful, intentional, and explicit oral language support.

During a 4th grade science lesson, here's how a teacher of students in the process of learning English might address explaining and communicating. Students pour water down an erosion tray and predict how the angle of the tray will affect the amount of erosion as measured by the sediment that collects in the tray. The teacher records this in the Task section of the Academic Language Framework (see Figure 11.2). The teacher then identifies the language function word in the task and records it in the Function of Language section. In this case, the function of language is predicting. Next, the teacher writes down what he expects students to say as they engage in discussion. What rich oral academic language would they use as they engage with one another to make predictions? He records one or two examples in the Exemplars area. In 4th grade, proficient speakers might be expected to say, "If the tray is at a greater angle, then more sediment will be washed away by the stream of water." Finally, the teacher decides what supports students learning English will need in order to engage at that level of academic talk. He records these items in the appropriate sections of the template:

- **Vocabulary**—key words needed to engage in the standard: *erosion, angle, sediment*
- **Grammar**—grammatical structures and parts of speech: *if . . . then*
- **Sentence starter**—"If the tray is at a ___angle, then ____ sediment will be washed away."

By identifying the function of language along with the vocabulary, grammar, and sentence starters for a lesson, the teacher is better able to support language learning in addition to content learning.

FIGURE 11.2
Academic Language Framework for a 4th Grade Science Lesson

Task	Exemplars	Academic Language			
		Function of Language	Vocabulary	Grammar	Sentence Starter(s)
Describe the relationship between the angle of water flowing down a slope and the amount of erosion.	"If the tray is at a greater angle, then more sediment will be washed away by the stream of water."	predicting	*erosion, angle, sediment*	if . . . then	If the tray is at a ___ angle, then ____ sediment will be washed away.

Tips for Teaching Using Generating and Testing Hypotheses

- Remember there are four processes for generating and testing hypotheses—systems analysis, problem solving, experimental inquiry, and investigation—and all of them provide numerous opportunities for students to talk about their learning and thinking. Be PIE (purposeful, intentional, and explicit) about incorporating all four into lesson design and delivery.

- Listen to the talking that occurs in the small collaborative groups you have purposefully planned. Listen for academic language and not conversational language. Academic talk is characterized by longer and more complex sentences with higher-level vocabulary.
- Remember to incorporate the S part of the Word-MES formula to help students sound like a book.

Conclusion

As we noted in the introduction, the number of English language learners (and others in need of language development) in U.S. classrooms continues to increase. For the most part, mainstream teachers are now responsible for helping these students learn English and master the required academic content. Are teachers prepared, however, to meet the needs of this population, particularly given the increased rigor the Common Core State Standards are likely to bring to their classrooms?

Available data indicate that, for the most part, few mainstream teachers are prepared to work with English language learners. A 2008 study from the National Clearinghouse of English Language Acquisition found that although most teachers have at least one English language learner in their classrooms, only 29.5 percent are trained to teach students in need of language development effectively, and only 20 states require that all teachers be trained to work with English language learners (Ballantyne, Sanderman, & Levy, 2008).

It's our hope that this book will help fill that gap for you and all of the students in your classroom who are in need of language development, whatever their native languages. You and all of your students deserve days filled with rich learning experiences in which you, the teacher, feel confident that you have modified and adapted your teaching strategies in ways that will allow your students to experience success in the classroom and beyond.

Appendix A:
The Academic Language Framework

Task	Exemplars	Academic Language			
		Function of Language	Vocabulary	Grammar	Sentence Starter(s)

Appendix B:
Thinking Language Matrix

Levels of Thinking and Language Functions	Tiered Thinking Across Stages of Second-Language Acquisition				
Level of thinking and academic language required for any task; move from concrete recall to more complex, abstract levels.	Language moves from simple to complex in grammatical tenses, forms, vocabulary, etc.				
	WORD ⟶ MODEL ⟶ EXPAND ⟶ SOUND LIKE A BOOK				
	Preproduction: nonverbal response	**Early Production:** one-word response	**Speech Emergence:** phrases or short sentences	**Intermediate Fluency:** longer and more complex sentences	**Advanced Fluency:** near native
Evaluation appraise, argue, assess, attach, choose, compare, defend, estimate, evaluate, judge, predict, rate, select, support, value					
Synthesis arrange, assemble, collect, compose, construct, create, design, develop, formulate, manage, organize, plan, prepare, propose, set up					

	WORD ⟶ MODEL ⟶ EXPAND ⟶ SOUND LIKE A BOOK				
	Preproduction: nonverbal response	Early Production: one-word response	Speech Emergence: phrases or short sentences	Intermediate Fluency: longer and more complex sentences	Advanced Fluency: near native
Analysis analyze, appraise, calculate, categorize, compare, contrast, criticize, differentiate, discriminate, distinguish, examine, experiment, question, test					
Application apply, choose, demonstrate, dramatize, employ, illustrate, interpret, operate, practice, schedule, sketch, solve, use					
Comprehension classify, describe, discuss, explain, express, identify, indicate, locate, recognize, report, restate, review, select, translate					
Knowledge arrange, define, describe, duplicate, label, list, name, order, recall, recognize, relate, repeat, reproduce, state					

Source: From *Classroom Instruction That Works with English Language Learners: Participant's Workbook* (p. 93), by J. D. Hill and C. L. Björk, 2008, Alexandria, VA: ASCD. Copyright 2008 by McREL. Adapted with permission.

Appendix C:
Template for Planning Language Objectives

STEP 1: Determine the Language Functions		
Language Function	**General Examples**	**Specific Examples**
• What is the purpose for communication in this lesson? • What does the learner have to accomplish with the language?	to name, to describe, to classify, to compare, to explain, to predict, to infer, to suggest, to evaluate, to request,	

STEP 2: Determine the Language Structures *(Choose 1, 2, or all 3 parts.)*		
Language Structure	**General Examples**	**Specific Examples**
1. Sentence Starters: What is the phrasing needed? What is an appropriate sentence frame?	• This is a _____. • The ___ lives in _____. • I believe ___ is going to ___ because ___.	
2. Key Words: What are some important vocabulary words or terms?	• Content vocabulary for objects, places, measurements, time • Prepositions, adjectives • Connectors (*although, as soon as, on the day that*)	
3. Minilesson: How can you use grammar in an authentic context?	• Command form of verbs • Simple future for prediction • (___ *is going to* + verb) • Word order • Idioms	

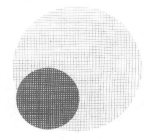

Appendix D:
Sample Graphic Organizers

Chronological Sequece

Objective: Learn to use the text as written, accompanying graphic organizer, and signal words to form a summary.

Questions
1. What sequence is being described? *History of technology in schools*
2. What are are the major incidents that occur? *1983—Apple II computer* *1999—interactive whiteboards* *2005—iclicker* *2006—laptops* *2010—iPads* Use your answers to these questions to form a summary.

Signal Words				
after	afterward	as soon as	before	during
finally	first	following	for (duration)	immediately
initially	later	meanwhile	next	not long after
now	on (date)	proceeding	second	soon
then	third	today	until	when

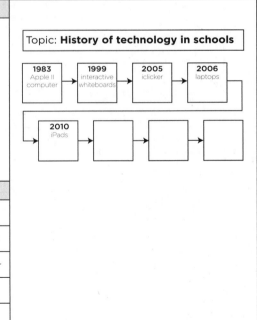

Summary: In 1983, Apple II computers found widespread acceptance in education with computer-based tutorials and learning games. The next major advancement was interactive whiteboards in 1999, followed by the iclicker in 2005. Not long after, laptops appeared, and finally, iPads.

Compare/Contrast Patterns
Secondary Social Studies

Objective: Learn to use the text as written, accompanying graphic organizer, and signal words to form a summary.

Questions

1. What items are being compared?
   Education, health care, and national security

2. What is it about them that is being compared; what general characteristics of the items form the basis of the comparison?
   Role of government

3. What characteristics do they have in common; how are these items alike?
   Issues in the election with party lines

4. In what way(s) are these items different?
   Issues involve different branches of the government and parts of society

5. What conclusion does the author reach about the degree of similarity or difference between the items?
   Author concludes the role of government is different

Use your answers to these questions to form a summary.

Signal Words			
although	as well as	as opposed to	both
but	compared	different from	either . . . or
even though	however	likewise	on the other hand
otherwise	similar to	similarly	still
whereas	yet	rather than	equivalent

Obama **Romney**

HOW ALIKE?

More early education

HOW DIFFERENT?

WITH REGARD TO

Wants government-suported program	Health Care
Want to reduce troops in the Middle East	National Security

Wants private program

Want more troops in the Middle East

Summary: Although both candidates had commonalities regarding education, the biggest differences are on health care and national security.

Concept/Definition Pattern
High School PE

Objective: Learn to use the text as written, accompanying graphic organizer, and signal words to form a summary.

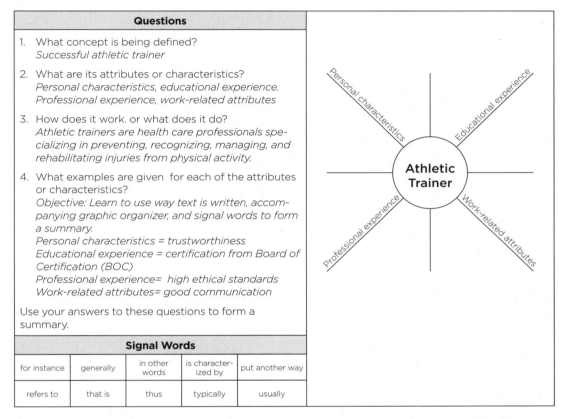

Questions
1. What concept is being defined? *Successful athletic trainer*
2. What are its attributes or characteristics? *Personal characteristics, educational experience.* *Professional experience, work-related attributes*
3. How does it work. or what does it do? *Athletic trainers are health care professionals specializing in preventing, recognizing, managing, and rehabilitating injuries from physical activity.*
4. What examples are given for each of the attributes or characteristics? *Objective: Learn to use way text is written, accompanying graphic organizer, and signal words to form a summary.* *Personal characteristics = trustworthiness* *Educational experience = certification from Board of Certification (BOC)* *Professional experience= high ethical standards* *Work-related attributes= good communication*
Use your answers to these questions to form a summary.

Signal Words				
for instance	generally	in other words	is characterized by	put another way
refers to	that is	thus	typically	usually

Summary: Being a successful athletic trainer depends on many factors. In addition to board certification, a trainer must be trustworthy. Besides having professional experience demonstrating high ethical standards, a trainer needs to be a good communicator.

Description Pattern
High School Social Studies

Objective: Learn to use the text as written, accompanying graphic organizer, and signal words to form a summary.

Questions
1. What specific person, place, thing, or event is being described? *Pacific theater of WWII*
2. What are the most important attributes or characteristics? *Fighting on island vs. large land mass/continent, more naval and air involvement. Fighting Japan, who we hadn't been to war with before.*
3. Why are these particular attributes important or significant? *They represent different conditions and attitude/culture.*
4. Why is this important? *Because it enlightens us about WWII and the war in Pacific.*
Use your answers to these questions to form a summary.

Signal Words			
above	across	along	appears to be
as in	behind	below	beside
between	down	in back of	in front of
looks like	near	next to	on top of
onto	outside	over	such as
to the right/left	under	adjectives	adverbs

Graphic organizer showing "Pacific Theater WWII" in the center connected to:
- Ended August 15, 1945
- Began 12/7/41 Pearl Harbor
- Battles for small islands
- Battles in unfamiliar territory
- Pacific war in addition to European land war

Summary: U.S. went to war with Japan as a result of the bombing of Pearl Harbor, December 7, 1941. This war was different than a land-based war because it involved many unfamiliar islands and an enemy we had never encountered.

Episode Pattern
5th Grade History

Objective: Learn to use the text as written, accompanying graphic organizer, and signal words to form a summary.

Questions

1. What event is being explained or described?
   Boston Tea Party

2. What is the setting where the events occurs?
   Boston Harbor, Boston Massachusetts.

3. When did these events occur?
   1773

4. Who are the major figures or characters that play a part in this?
   British Parliament
   East India Tea Company
   The Activists

5. List the order they occur, the specific incidents or events.
   - *British Parliament passes the Tea Act granting the East India Tea Company a monopoly on trade*
   - *People of Boston meet*
   - *Sons of Liberty dump tea into the harbor disguised as Indians*
   - *Aftermath led to American Revolution*

6. What caused this event?
   British Parliament thought the colonists were not acting as a colony should act.

7. What effects did this event have on the people involved?
   Hardened the positions on each side.

8. What effects has this event had on society in general?
   Laid the foundation for protesting unfair treatment by the government.

Use your answers to these questions to form a summary.

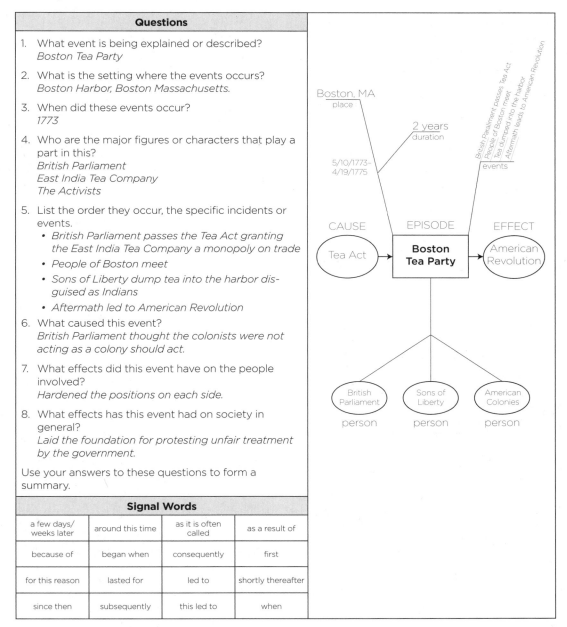

Signal Words			
a few days/ weeks later	around this time	as it is often called	as a result of
because of	began when	consequently	first
for this reason	lasted for	led to	shortly thereafter
since then	subsequently	this led to	when

Summary: The British Parliament passed the Tea Act to assert their power. Subsequently, the Sons of Liberty dumped tea into the harbor. As a result of this incident, the colonies and England went to war.

Generalization/Principle Pattern
4th Grade History

Objective: Learn to use the text as written, accompanying graphic organizer, and signal words to form a summary.

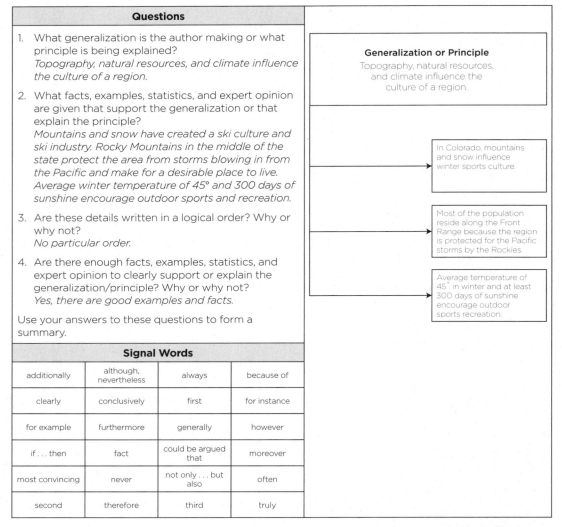

Questions
1. What generalization is the author making or what principle is being explained? *Topography, natural resources, and climate influence the culture of a region.*
2. What facts, examples, statistics, and expert opinion are given that support the generalization or that explain the principle? *Mountains and snow have created a ski culture and ski industry. Rocky Mountains in the middle of the state protect the area from storms blowing in from the Pacific and make for a desirable place to live. Average winter temperature of 45° and 300 days of sunshine encourage outdoor sports and recreation.*
3. Are these details written in a logical order? Why or why not? *No particular order.*
4. Are there enough facts, examples, statistics, and expert opinion to clearly support or explain the generalization/principle? Why or why not? *Yes, there are good examples and facts.*

Use your answers to these questions to form a summary.

Generalization or Principle
Topography, natural resources, and climate influence the culture of a region.

In Colorado, mountains and snow influence winter sports culture.

Most of the population reside along the Front Range because the region is protected for the Pacific storms by the Rockies.

Average temperature of 45° in winter and at least 300 days of sunshine encourage outdoor sports recreation.

Signal Words			
additionally	although, nevertheless	always	because of
clearly	conclusively	first	for instance
for example	furthermore	generally	however
if . . . then	fact	could be argued that	moreover
most convincing	never	not only . . . but also	often
second	therefore	third	truly

Summary: The topography, natural resources, and climate of the region influence the culture. For example, in Colorado, the mountains and snow have created a ski culture and ski industry. Futhermore, the excellent weather promotes "outdoorism." Additionally, the high Rockies block adverse weather conditions for the majority of the population along the Front Range.

References

Alanis, I. (2004). Effective instruction: Integrating language and literacy. In C. Salinas (Ed.), *Scholars in the field: The challenge of migrant education* (pp. 211–224). Charleston, WV: Appalachian Regional Education Laboratory.

Anstrom, K., DiCerbo, P., Butler, F., Katz, A., Millet, J., & Rivera, C. (2010). *A review of the literature on academic English: Implications for K–12 English language learners.* Arlington, VA: George Washington University Center for Equity and Excellence in Education.

Asher, J. J. (1969). The total physical response approach to second language learning. *Modern Language Journal, 53*(1), 3–17.

August, D., & Shanahan, T. (Eds.). (2006). *Developing literacy in second-language learners: Report of the National Literacy Panel on Language-Minority Children and Youth* (Executive Summary). Mahwah, NJ: Lawrence Erlbaum Associates.

Ballantyne, K. G., Sanderman, A. R., & Levy, J. (2008). Educating English language learners: Building teacher capacity. Washington, DC: National Clearinghouse for English Language Acquisition. Available at http://www.ncela.gwu.edu/files/uploads/3/EducatingELLsBuildingTeacherCapacityVol1.pdf

Beck, I. L., McKeown, M. G., & Kucan, I. (2002). *Bringing words to life: Robust vocabulary instruction.* New York: Guilford Press.

Beesley, A. D., & Apthorp, H. S. (2010). *Classroom instruction that works, second edition: Research report.* Denver, CO: Mid-continent Research for Education and Learning.

Berman, P., Minicucci, C., McLaughlin, B., Nelson, B., & Woodworth, K. (1995). *School reform and student diversity: Case studies of exemplary practices for LEP students.* Washington, DC: National Clearinghouse for English Language Acquisition.

Block, C. C., Gambrell, L., & Pressley, M. (2002). *Improving comprehension instruction: Rethinking research, theory, and classroom practice.* San Francisco: Jossey-Bass.

Bloom, B. S., Engelhart, M. D., Furst, E. J., Hill, W. H., & Krathwohl, D. R. (Eds). (1956). *Taxonomy of educational objectivities: The classification of educational goals. Handbook I: Cognitive domain.* New York: David McKay.

Brophy, J. (2004). *Motivating students to learn* (2nd ed.). Boston: McGraw-Hill.

Cochran, C. (1989). *Strategies for involving LEP students in the all-English medium classroom: A cooperative learning approach.* NCELA Program Information Guide Series (No. 12).

Coley, J. D., & DePinto, T. (1989). *Reciprocal teaching: Theme and variations.* (ERIC Document Reproduction Service No. ED 308 477)

Collier, V. P., & Thomas, W. P. (1989). How quickly can immigrants become proficient in school English? *Journal of Educational Issues of Language Minority Students, 5,* 26–38.

Council of Chief State Officers. (2010). *Common core state standards initiative.* Retrieved from http://www.corestandards.org/

Council of Chief State School Officers. (2012). *Framework for English language proficiency development standards corresponding to the Common Core State Standards and the Next Generation Science Standards.* Washington, DC: CCSSO.

Cummins, J. (1984). *Bilingualism and special education: Issues in assessment and pedagogy.* San Diego, CA: College-Hill Press.

De Jong, E. J., & Harper, C. A. (2005, Spring). Preparing mainstream teachers for English-language learners: Is being a good teacher good enough? *Teacher Education Quarterly, 32*(2), 101–124.

Dean, C. B., Hubbell, E. R., Pitler, H., & Stone, B. (2012). *Classroom instruction that works* (2nd ed.). Alexandria, VA: ASCD.

Dresser, N. (1996). *Multicultural manners.* Toronto: Wiley.

Duke, N. K., & Pearson, P. (2002). Effective practices for developing reading comprehension. In A. E. Farstrup & S. Samuels (Eds.), *What research has to say about reading instruction* (pp. 205–242). Newark, DE: International Reading Association.

Englander, K. (2002, January). Real life problem solving: A collaborative learning activity. *English Teaching Forum, 40*(1), 8–12.

Fathman, A. K., Quinn, M. E., & Kessler, C. (1992). Teaching science to English learners, grades 4–8. *NCELA Program Information Guide Series, 11,* 1–27.

Fillippone, M. (1998). *Questioning at the elementary level* (Master's thesis, Kean University). (ERIC Document Reproduction Service No. ED 417 421)

Fillmore, L. W., & Snow, C. E. (2000). *What teachers need to know about language.* (ERIC Clearinghouse on Languages and Linguistics Special Report). Washington, DC: Office of Educational Research and Improvement (Center for Applied Linguistics).

Fisher, D., & Frey, N. (2008). *Better learning through structured teaching: A framework for the gradual release of responsibility.* Alexandria, VA: ASCD.

Freeman, Y. S., & Freeman, D. E. (2009). *Academic language for English language learners and struggling readers.* Portsmouth, NH: Heinemann.

Gibbons, P. (1991). *Learning to learn in a second language.* Portsmouth, NH: Heinemann.

Gibbons, P. (2006). *Bridging discourses in the ESL classroom: Students, teachers and researchers.* London: Continuum.

Harper, C., & de Jong, E. (2004). Misconceptions about teaching English-language learners. *Journal of Adolescent & Adult Literacy, 48*(2), 152–161.

Henderlong, J., & Lepper, M. R. (2002). The effects of praise on student motivation: A review and synthesis. *Psychological Bulletin, 128,* 774–795.

Herrera, S. C., Perez, D. R., & Escamilla, K. (2010). *Teaching reading to English language learners.* Boston: Allyn and Bacon.

Hill, J. D., & Björk, C. L. (2008a). *Classroom instruction that works with English language learners facilitator's guide.* Alexandria, VA: ASCD.

Hill, J. D., & Björk, C. L. (2008b). *Classroom instruction that works with English language learners participant's workbook.* Alexandria, VA: ASCD.

Hill, J. D., & Flynn, K. (2006). *Classroom instruction that works with English language learners* (1st ed.). Alexandria, VA: ASCD.

Hill, J. D., & Hoak, H. (2012). *English language learner resource guide: Top ten instructional tips for schools with a low incidence of ELLs.* Denver, CO: Mid-continent Research for Education and Learning.

Himmele, P., & Himmele, W. (2011). *Total participation techniques.* Alexandria, VA: ASCD.

Hong, E., Milgram, R. M., & Rowell, L. L. (2004). Homework motivation and preference: A learner-centered homework approach. *Theory into Practice, 43*(3), 197–204.

Johnson, D. W., & Johnson, F. P. (2009). *Joining together* (10th ed.). Upper Saddle River, NJ: Pearson.

Johnson, D. W., & Johnson, R. T. (1999). *Learning together and alone: Cooperative, competitive, and individualistic learning.* Boston: Allyn and Bacon.

Johnson, D. W., & Johnson, R. T. (2009). An educational psychology success story: Social interdependence theory and cooperative learning. *Educational Research, 38*(5), 365–379.

Johnson, D. W., Johnson, R. T., & Holubec, E. (1998). *Cooperation in the classroom.* Boston: Allyn and Bacon.

Jones, B. F., Palincsar, A. S., Ogle, D. S., & Carr, E. G. (1987). *Strategic teaching and learning: Cognitive instruction in the content areas.* Alexandria, VA: ASCD.

Kagan, S. (1992). *Cooperative learning.* San Juan Capistrano, CA: Resources for Teachers Inc.

Kagan, S. (1995). *We can talk: Cooperative learning in the elementary ESL classroom.* (ERIC Document Reproduction Service No. ED 382 035)

Kamins, M. L., & Dweck, C. S. (1999). Person versus process praise and criticism: Implications for contingent self-worth and coping. *Developmental Psychology, 35,* 835–847.

Karpicke, J. D., & Roediger III, H. R. (2008). The critical importance of retrieval for learning, *Science, 319,* 966–968.

Kathpalia, S. S., & Carmel, H. L. H. (2011). Metaphorical competence in ESL student writing. *RELC Journal, 42*(3), 273–290.

Kauffman, D. (2007). *What's different about teaching reading to students learning English.* McHenry, IL: Delta Publishing Company.

Klem, A. M., & Connell, J. P. (2004). Relationships matter: Linking teacher support to student engagement and achievement. *Journal of School Health, 74*(7), 262–273.

Krashen, S. D., & Terrell, T. (1983). *The natural approach: Language acquisition in the classroom.* Oxford: Pergamon.

Marzano, R. J., & Pickering, D. J. (1997). *Dimensions of learning.* Alexandria, VA: ASCD.

Marzano, R. J., Pickering, D. J., & Pollock, J. E. (2001). *Classroom instruction that works* (1st ed.). Alexandria, VA: ASCD.

McDaniel, M. A., Roediger, H. L., & McDermott, K. B. (2007). Addressing nonscientific presuppositions in genetics using a conceptual change strategy. *Science Education, 91*(3), 419–438.

Medina, J. (2008). *Brain rules: 12 principles for surviving and thriving at work, home, and school.* Seattle, WA: Pear Press.

Minotti, J. L. (2005). Effects of learning style–based homework prescriptions on the achievement and attitudes of middle school students. *NASSP Bulletin, 89*(642), 67–89.

Moore-Partin, T. C., Robertson, R. E., Maggin, D. M., Oliver, R. M., & Wehby, J. H. (2012). Using teacher praise and opportunities to respond to appropriate student behavior. *Preventing School Failure, 54.*

Next Generation Science Standards. (2012). Retrieved from http://www.nextgenscience.org/

Oliver, R. (2003). Interactional context and feedback in child ESL classrooms. *The Modern Language Journal, 87,* 519–533.

Ovando, C. J., Collier, V. P., & Combs, M. C. (2003). *Bilingual and ESL classrooms.* New York: McGraw-Hill.

Paivio, A. (2006). Dual coding theory and education. Draft chapter for the conference on "Pathways to Literacy Achievement for High Poverty Children," University of Michigan School of Education, September 29–October 1, 2006. Retrieved from www.umich.edu/~rdytolrn/pathwaysconference/presentations/paivio.pdf

Rader, H. (n.d.). *A sponge is a summary.* Retrieved from: http://www.choiceliteracy.com/articles-detail-view.php?id=736

Ramirez, J. S. (1992). Executive summary of the final report: Longitudinal study of structured English immersion, strategy, early-exit and late-exit transitional bilingual education programs for language minority children. *Bilingual Research Journal, 16*(1–2), 1–62.

Saunders, W. & Goldenberg, C. (2010). Research to guide English language development instruction. In *Improving Education for English Learners: Research-Based Approaches* (pp. 21–81). Sacramento, CA: State Department of Education.

Saunders, W. M., & O'Brien, G. (2006). Oral language. In F. Genesse, K. Lindholm-Leary, W. M. Saunders, & D. Christian (Eds.), *Educating English language learners: A synthesis of research evidence* (pp. 14–63). New York: Cambridge University Press.

Schoen, F., & Schoen, A. A. (2003). Action research in the classroom. *Teaching Exceptional Children, 35*(3), 16–21.

Short, D. (1991) Integrating language and content instruction: Strategies and techniques. *NCELA Program Information Guide Series, Number 7,* 1–23.

Short, D. J. (1994). Study examines role of academic language in social studies content-ESL classes. *Forum, 17*(3).

Stone, B., & Urquhart, V. (2008). *Remove limits to learning with systematic vocabulary instruction.* Denver, CO: Mid-continent Research for Education and Learning.

Thomas, W. P. & Collier, V. P. (1997, December). *School effectiveness for language minority students.* National Clearinghouse for English Language Acquisition (NCELA) Resource Collection Series, No. 9.

Urquhart, V., & Frazee, D. (2012). *Teaching reading in the content areas: If not me, then who?* (3rd ed.). Alexandria, VA: ASCD.

U.S. Department of Education. (n.d). Ed Data Express: Data about elementary and secondary schools in the U.S. National Student Demographics. Retrieved from: http://www.eddataexpress.ed.gov/state-report.cfm?state=US&submit.x=25&submit.y=7

Understanding Language. (n.d.). *Overview.* Retrieved from: http://ell.stanford.edu/about.

Vygotsky, L. S. (1978). *Mind in society: The development of higher psychological processes.* Cambridge, MA: Harvard University Press.

Walqui, A. (2010, January 30). *Defining quality teaching for English learners: Principals and practices.* Paper presented at the Third Annual ACOE English Learner Conference—Advancing the Language and Literacy of English Learners.

Walqui, A. (2012). *Common core standards and English language learners: Affordances and challenges.* Retrieved from http://www.calsa.org/wp-content/uploads/2012/01/Aida-Walqui.pdf

Wilhelm, J. D. (2001). *Improving comprehension with think-aloud strategies.* New York: Scholastic.

Williams, C., & Roberts, D. (2011). Strategic oral language instruction in ELD. Brea, CA: Ballard & Tighe. Retrieved from http://www.ballard-tighe.com/pdfs/fff/whitepaper_email.pdf

Williams, C., Stathis, R., & Gotsch, P. (2009). Speaking of writing. *Language Magazine, 8,* 20–22.

Wormeli, R. (2009). *Metaphors and analogies: Power tools for teaching any subject.* Portland, ME: Stenhouse Publishers.

Zehler, A. (1994, Summer). Working with English language learners: Strategies for elementary and middle school teachers. *NCELA Program Information Guide Series, 19.*

Index

The letter *f* following a page number denotes a figure.

Academic Language Framework, using the, 6–8, 7*f*
Academic Language Framework examples
  Common Core State Standards for Mathematics addressed using, 62–63, 63*f*, 110, 111*f*
  compare similarities and differences, 148*f*
  English Language Arts standards addressed using, 6, 7*f*
  hypotheses, generating and testing, 157*f*
  Next Generation Science Standards addressed, 96–98, 97*f*
  teaching content and language, 30, 30*f*
Academic Language Framework template, 161
accountability, individual, 53–55
achievement and effort. *See also* effort, reinforcing
  linking, 38–39
  in oral academic language development, 45
  student tracking to reinforce, 42–43, 43*f*
  Thinking Language Matrix for, 44–45*f*
achievement and effort rubric, 43*f*
advanced fluency stage
  characteristics, 12*f*, 13
  tiered questions and time frame, 12*f*
advance organizers
  classroom practice recommendations, 76–81
  expository type, 77
  graphic type, 80–81

advance organizers (*continued*)
  narrative type, 77–78, 79
  in oral academic language development, 83–85
  skimming used as, 78, 80
  teaching tips, 85–86
  Thinking Language Matrix for, 82*f*
analogies, creating, 135, 141–143
Analysis level, Bloom's taxonomy, 75, 123, 145–146
analytic questions, 70
Application level, Bloom's taxonomy, 28–29, 29*f*, 129
attribute charts, 136, 139
Author and You questions, 75

basic interpersonal communicative skills (BICS), 1, 19. *See also* conversational language development
BICS (basic interpersonal communicative skills), 1, 19. *See also* conversational language development
Bloom's taxonomy
  Analysis level, 75, 123, 145–146
  Application level, 28–29, 29*f*, 129
  Comprehension level, 82
  critical thinking levels aligned to, 17
  Evaluation level, 59–61, 60*f*, 93, 94*f*
  QAR strategy and, 76*f*
  questions, linking to, 17, 75, 76*f*, 85
  second language acquisition stages relationship, 19*f*

Bloom's taxonomy (*continued*)
  Synthesis level, 108, 115
CALP (cognitive academic language
  proficiency), 20
chronological sequence pattern
  graphic organizer example, 165
  signal words and, 5–6, 102

Classifying Memory Game, 146–147, 146*f*
classify similarities and differences, 135,
  139–140
cognitive academic language proficiency
  (CALP), 20
combination notes, 113, 113*f*
Common Core Mathematical Practice Standard
  I, 9
Common Core State Standards for language
  arts and literacy in history/social studies, 129
Common Core State Standards for
  Mathematics, 62–63, 63*f*, 110, 111*f*, 123
compare/contrast pattern
  graphic organizer example, 166
  signal words and, 102
  Thinking Language Matrix examples,
    129–130, 129*f*
compare similarities and differences, 135,
  136–138, 148*f*
Comprehension level, Bloom's taxonomy, 82
concept/definition pattern
  graphic organizer example, 167
  signal words and, 102
content objectives
  communicating to parents, 27
  language objectives and, 30
  setting, 30, 30*f*, 36
conversational language development. *See also*
  basic interpersonal communicative skills
  (BICS)
  example, 4
  in feedback, 33, 56
  iceberg concept of, 19–20
  sentence starters for, 44
  signal words and, 103
  writing for, 2, 126–127
cooperative learning
  advantages of, 53
  classroom practice recommendations,
    53–58
  consistent and systematic use, 57

cooperative learning (*continued*)
  elements differentiating, 52
  individual accountability in, 53–55
  informal, 57, 58–59*f*
  positive interdependence in, 53–55
  reciprocal teaching for, 64, 117
  small group size for, 55–57
  teaching tips, 63–65
  types of groupings for, 57
Council of Chief State School Officers (English
  Language Proficiency Development
  Framework), 9
critical thinking levels, 17–19
cues. *See also* questions
  classroom practice recommendations,
    68–71
  explicit, using, 68–70, 69*f*
  focus of, 68
  function of, 67
  percent of student-teacher interactions,
    67
  teaching tips, 85–86
  Thinking Language Matrix for, 71–75,
    73–74*f*
culture
  iceberg concept of, 49*f*, 51
  praise and recognition in context of, 49*f*,
    48, 50

description pattern
  graphic organizer example, 168
  signal words and, 102
dual-coding theory, 86–87

early production stage
  characteristics, 12*f*, 13
  tiered questions and time frame, 12*f*
effort, reinforcing
  classroom practice recommendations,
    38–42
  by explicit explanation of expending
    effort, 39–42, 41*f*, 42*f*
  linking to achievement for, 38–39
  in oral academic language development,
    45
  by student tracking of, 42–43, 43*f*
  teaching tips, 50–51
  Thinking Language Matrix for, 44–45*f*
effort rubric, 41*f*

effort, reinforcing (*continued*)
English Language Arts standard, 6, 7*f*
English language development, types of
   students requiring, xi
English Language Learner Resource Guide (Hill &
   Hoak), 124
English Language Learners, percent of student
   population, xi
English Language Proficiency Development
   Framework (Council of Chief State School
   Officers), 9
episode pattern
      graphic organizer example, 169
      signal words and, 102
Evaluation level, Bloom's taxonomy, 59–61,
   60*f*, 93, 94*f*
expository advance organizers, 77–78
expository text, function of, 101

feedback
      for addressing what is correct, 31
      classroom practice recommendations,
         31–33
      in conversational language development,
         33, 56
      criterion referenced, 32
      for elaborating on what to do next, 31
      engaging students in the process, 32–33
      on homework, 122
      in oral academic language development,
         35
      practice activity example, 128
      small group size for, 56
      teaching tips, 36–37
      Thinking Language Matrix for, 33–34, 34*f*
      time frame for, 31–32
Four Corners, 58*f*, 59–61, 60*f*

generalization/principle pattern
      graphic organizer example, 170
      signal words and, 102–103
gradual release of responsibility model, 93
graphic advance organizers, 80–81
graphic organizers
      chronological sequence, 165
      compare/contrast patterns, 166
      concept/definition pattern, 167
      description pattern, 168
      episode pattern, 169

graphic organizers (*continued*)
      generalization/principle pattern, 170
      as nonlinguistic representations, 87–88
      summary formulation using, 103

homework
      classroom practice recommendations,
         118–122
      communicating purpose with, 120–122
      feedback on, 122
      incorporating language objectives, 119
      in oral academic language development,
         124
      school/district policy, develop and
         communicate on, 119
      supporting academic learning using,
         120–122
      teaching tips, 130–131
      Thinking Language Matrix for, 123*f*
hypotheses, generating and testing
      classroom practice recommendations,
         151–154
      by engaging students in structured tasks,
         151–153
      in oral academic language development,
         156–157, 157*f*
      process, 150
      student explanations in, 153–154
      teaching tips, 157–158
      Thinking Language Matrix for, 154–156

iceberg concept of culture, 49*f*, 51
illustrations as nonlinguistic representations,
   90
inferential questions, 70
informational text
      function of, 101
      patterns and signal words, 102–103
Inside-Outside Circle, 59*f*
intermediate fluency stage
      characteristics, 12*f*, 13
      tiered questions and time frame, 12*f*

kinesthetic activities, 91–92, 100–101
knowledge, methods of storing, 86
K-W-L charts, 68–70, 69*f*
language, conversational vs. academic, 5–6
language functions, 2–5
language objectives

connecting to previous and future
learning, 28
feedback's use in, 31
function of, 36
incorporating into homework, 119
teaching tips, 36–37
Language Objectives Planning Template, 26,
27f, 164
language structures, 2, 3–5
learning objectives
classroom practice recommendations,
25–28
communicating to students and parents,
26–27
connecting to previous and future
learning, 28
homework aligned to, 120–122
practice activities aligned to, 124–125
specific but not restrictive, 25–26
teaching tips, 36–37
Thinking Language Matrix for, 28–29, 29f

manipulatives as nonlinguistic representations,
88–89
mental pictures as nonlinguistic
representations, 89–90
metaphors, creating, 135, 140–141, 143–144
On My Own questions, 75

narrative advance organizers, 77–78, 79
National Clearinghouse of English Language
Acquisition, 159
National Literacy Panel on Language, 130
The Natural Approach (Krashen & Terrell), 11
Next Generation Science Standards, 71–72, 96,
97f, 147–148
No Child Left Behind Act, 13
nonlinguistic representations
classroom practice recommendations,
87–92
combination notes as, 113, 113f
comparing similarities and differences,
138
graphic organizers as, 87–88
illustrations, 90
kinesthetic activities as, 91–92
knowledge stored using, 86–87
manipulatives, 88–89
mental pictures as, 89–90

nonlinguistic representations (continued)
metaphors and, 140–141
in oral academic language development,
95–96, 97f
physical models as, 88–89
pictographs as, 90
pictures as, 90–91
teaching tips, 93
Thinking Language Matrix for, 92–95, 94f
using all senses, 89–90
webbing, 112–113
note taking
classroom practice recommendations,
111–114
formats for, teaching, 112–113
in oral academic language development,
116–117
revise and review opportunities, 113–114
teacher-prepared notes for students,
111–112, 112f
teaching tips, 117
Thinking Language Matrix for, 114–116,
115f
Numbered Heads Together, 58f

oral academic language development
conversational language development
vs., 5–6
intentionality in, 61, 62–63
listening in, 61
Next Generation Science Standards
addressed, 147–148
percent of teachers trained in, 159
Word-MES strategy, 35, 36, 127–128, 158
writing's relationship to, 2, 126–127
oral academic language development
opportunities
advance organizers, 83–85
content and language, 29–30, 30f
effort-achievement relationship, 45
feedback, 35
focused practice example, 127
homework, 124
hypotheses, generating and testing,
156–157, 157f
nonlinguistic representations, 95–96, 97f
note taking, 116–117
practice activities, 130
QAR strategy, 75–76

oral academic language development
    opportunities (*continued*)
        similarities and differences, 147–148
        summarizing, 109–110

Paraphrase Passport, 59*f*
parent communications
    on homework policy, 119–120
    on learning objectives, 26–27
physical models as nonlinguistic
    representations, 88–89
pictographs as nonlinguistic representations,
    90
pictures as nonlinguistic representations, 90–91
practice activities
    classroom practice recommendations,
        124–128
    feedback and, 127–128
    identify and communicate purpose of,
        124–126
    in oral academic language development,
        130
    short, focused, and time distributed
        design, 126–127
    teaching tips, 130–131
praise, aligning with expectations, 49*f*, 47–48
preproduction stage
    characteristics, 12*f*, 13
    tiered questions and time frame, 12*f*

Question-Answer Relationships (QAR) strategy,
    72, 74–76, 76*f*
questions. *See also* cues; tiered questions
    analytic, 70
    Bloom's taxonomy and, 17, 75, 76*f*, 85
    classroom practice recommendations,
        68–71
    focus of, 68
    function of, 67
    inferential, 70
    knowledge-based, 74–75
    percent of student-teacher interactions,
        67
    teaching tips, 85–86
    text-based, 74–75
    Thinking Language Matrix for, 71–75,
        73–74*f*
    tiered, including students at all levels
        using, 18–19

questions. *See also* cues; tiered questions
    (*continued*)

reciprocal teaching
    for cooperative learning, 64, 117
    defined, 32
    for summarizing, 104–108
recognition
    aligning praise with expectations in, 49*f*
    classroom practice recommendations,
        46–50
    mastery-goal orientation, promote for,
        46, 47
    praise aligned with expectations in,
        47–48
    teaching tips, 50–51
    using concrete symbols, 48, 50
Review of the Literature on Academic English
    (Anstrom et al.), 1
Right There questions, 74
rule-based summarizing strategy, 99–101

scaffolding, 13–14
second-language acquisition, theories of, 1
second-language acquisition stages
    Bloom's taxonomy, linking to, 19*f*
    characteristics, by stage, 12*f*
    introduction, 11–14
    tiered questions, by stage, 12*f*
    time frame for, 12*f*, 19–20
the senses in nonlinguistic representation,
    89–90
sequence text pattern
    graphic organizer example, 165
    signal words and, 102
signal words, 5–6, 102–103
similarities and differences
    Academic Language Framework
        examples, 148*f*
    analogies, creating, 135, 141–143
    classifying, 135, 139–140
    classroom practice recommendations,
        136–138
    comparing, 135, 136–138
    guiding the process of identifying,
        143–144
    metaphors, creating, 135, 140–141,
        143–144

similarities and differences (*continued*)
    in oral academic language development,
       147–148
    stages of, 135
    supporting cues to identify, 144–145
    teaching tips, 149
    Thinking Language Matrix for, 145–147
skimming as an advance organizer, 78, 80
speech emergence stage
    characteristics, 12*f*, 13
    tiered questions and time frame, 12*f*
summarizing
    classroom practice recommendations,
       99–108
    effort checklist example, 42*f*
    reciprocal teaching for, 104–108
    rule-based strategy, teaching the, 99–101
    summary frames for, 101–104
    teaching tips, 117
    Thinking Language Matrix for, 108–109,
       109*f*
summarizing patterns
    compare/contrast, 102, 166
    concept/definition, 102, 167
    description, 102, 168
    episode, 102, 169
    generalization/principle, 102–103, 170
    sequence text, 102, 165
summary frames, 101–104
Synthesis level, Bloom's taxonomy, 108, 115

Teaching Reading in the Content Areas (Urquhart
    & Frazee), 101–102
text patterns and signal words, 101–103
Think and Search questions, 74–75
Thinking Language Matrix
    Classifying Memory Game, 146–147,
       146*f*
    Common Core State Standards addressed
       using, 129
    Four Corners activity, 59, 60*f*
    function, xiv
    Next Generation Science Standards
       addressed, 71–72
    using the, 8–10, 10*f*
Thinking Language Matrix-Bloom's taxonomy
    aligned

Thinking Language Matrix (*continued*)
    Analysis level, 123, 145–146
    Application level, 28–29, 29*f*, 129
    Comprehension level, 82
    Evaluation level, 59–61, 60*f*, 93, 94*f*
    Synthesis level, 108, 115
Thinking Language Matrix examples
    advance organizers, 82*f*
    cues and questions, 71–75, 73–74*f*
    effort-achievement relationship, 44–45*f*
    feedback, 33–34, 34*f*
    homework, 123*f*
    hypotheses, generating and testing,
       154–156, 155*f*
    learning objectives, setting, 28–29, 29*f*
    nonlinguistic representations, 92–95, 94*f*
    note taking, 114–116, 115*f*
    practice activities, 129–130, 129*f*
    summarizing, 108–109, 109*f*
Thinking Language Matrix template, 162–163
Three-Minute Review, 58*f*
Three-Step Interview, 58*f*
tiered questions. *See also* questions
    function of, 17
    including students at all levels using,
       14–16, 18–19
    ordering using Bloom's taxonomy, 17
    stages of second language acquisition
       and, 12*f*
    tiered, including students at all levels
       using, 18–19
tiered thinking, 17–19
time frame
    for feedback, 31–32
    for second-language acquisition, 12*f*,
       19–20
Total Physical Response (TPR), 91
transition words in informational text, 102–103

webbing, 112–113
Word-MES strategy, 35, 36, 127–128, 158
writing-language development relationship, 2,
    126–127

zone of proximal development, 13, 14

About the Authors

As a principal consultant for McREL, **Jane Hill** consults and trains teachers and administrators nationally and internationally. Her most recent endeavors involve training teachers in the Commonwealth of the Northern Mariana Islands for an ESL endorsement, writing two instructional guides for schools with a low incidence of English learners. Prior to joining McREL, she worked as a speech/language specialist focusing on bilingual special education, directed a two-way language school, and served as a district office director for second language acquisition and special education. She has worked in the areas of second language acquisition and special education for 35 years. Jane has published articles in *Language Magazine*, *The Journal of Staff Development*, *The School Administrator*, *Leadership Information*, and *Phi Delta Kappan*. She coauthored the first edition of *Classroom Instruction That Works with English Language Learners* and *Classroom Instruction That Works with English Language Learners Facilitator's Guide* and *Participant's Workbook*.

As a lead consultant in McREL's Communications depart-ment, **Kirsten Miller** writes and edits a wide range of reports, articles, and other publications. She has published articles in *Educational Leadership*, *ASCD Express*, *Principal Leadership*, *Phi Delta Kappan*, and *Principals Research Review*. Kirsten can be contacted at kmiller@mcrel.org.

About McREL

Mid-continent Research for Education and Learning (McREL) is a nationally recognized, nonprofit education research and development organization, headquartered in Denver, Colorado with offices in Honolulu, Hawai'i, and Melbourne, Australia. Since 1966, McREL has helped translate research and professional wisdom about what works in education into practical guidance for educators. Our 120-plus staff members and affiliates include respected researchers, experienced consultants, and published writers who provide educators with research-based guidance, consultation, and professional devel-opment for improving student outcomes. Contact us if you have questions or comments or would like to arrange a presentation, workshop, or other assistance from McREL in applying the ideas from this book in your district, school, or classroom.

Related ASCD Resources

At the time of publication, the following ASCD resources were available (ASCD stock numbers appear in parentheses). For up-to-date information about ASCD resources, go to www.ascd.org. You can search the complete archives of *Educational Leadership* at http://www.ascd.org/el.

Print Products

Classroom Instruction That Works: Research-Based Strategies for Increasing Student Achievement, 2nd Edition by Ceri B. Dean, Elizabeth Ross Hubbell, Howard Pitler, and Bj Stone (#111001)

Getting Started with English Language Learners: How Educators Can Meet the Challenge by Judie Haynes (#106048)

A Handbook for Classroom Instruction That Works, 2nd edition by Bj Stone and Howard Pitler (#112013)

How to Assess Higher-Order Thinking Skills in Your Classroom by Susan M. Brookhart (#109111)

The Language-Rich Classroom: A Research-Based Framework for Teaching English Language Learners by Pérsida Himmele and William Himmele (#108037)

Reaching Out to Latino Families of English Language Learners by David Campos, Mary Esther Huerta, and Rocio Delgado (#110005)

Teaching English Language Learners Across the Content Areas by Debbie E. Zacarian and Judie Haynes (#109032)

Using Technology with Classroom Instruction That Works, 2nd edition by Matt Kuhn, Elizabeth R. Hubbell, and Howard Pitler (#112012)

THE WHOLE CHILD The Whole Child Initiative helps schools and communities create learning environments that allow students to be healthy, safe, engaged, supported, and challenged. To learn more about other books and resources that relate to the whole child, visit www.wholechildeducation.org.

For more information: send e-mail to member@ascd.org; call 1-800-933-2723 or 703-578-9600, press 2; send a fax to 703-575-5400; or write to Information Services, ASCD, 1703 N. Beauregard St., Alexandria, VA 22311-1714 USA.

WHOLE CHILD
TENETS

1 **HEALTHY**
Each student enters school healthy and learns about and practices a healthy lifestyle.

2 **SAFE**
Each student learns in an environment that is physically and emotionally safe for students and adults.

3 **ENGAGED**
Each student is actively engaged in learning and is connected to the school and broader community.

4 **SUPPORTED**
Each student has access to personalized learning and is supported by qualified, caring adults.

5 **CHALLENGED**
Each student is challenged academically and prepared for success in college or further study and for employment and participation in a global environment.

THE WHOLE CHILD

The ASCD Whole Child approach is an effort to transition from a focus on narrowly defined academic achievement to one that promotes the long-term development and success of all children. Through this approach, ASCD supports educators, families, community members, and policymakers as they move from a vision about educating the whole child to sustainable, collaborative actions.

Classroom Instruction That Works, 2nd edition relates to the **engaged**, **supported**, and **challenged** tenets. *For more about the ASCD Whole Child approach, visit* **www.ascd.org/wholechild.**